"When Sister Thea was asked what she understood her vocation to be about, she confidently replied, 'I'm a teacher.' Hers was a lifetime of education, growing into the incredible person of faith God called her to be. Maurice Nutt masterfully presents the uncompromising message and unsurpassable life of Thea Bowman, his professor and friend. Looking to learn from life's teachable moments? Let Thea's class begin!"

—Byron Miller, CSsR, President, Liguori Publications

People of God

Remarkable Lives, Heroes of Faith

People of God is a series of inspiring biographies for the general reader. Each volume offers a compelling and honest narrative of the life of an important twentieth- or twenty-first-century Catholic. Some living and some now deceased, each of these women and men has known challenges and weaknesses familiar to most of us but responded to them in ways that call us to our own forms of heroism. Each offers a credible and concrete witness of faith, hope, and love to people of our own day.

John XXIII	Massimo Faggioli
Oscar Romero	Kevin Clarke
Thomas Merton	Michael W. Higgins
Francis	Michael Collins
Flannery O'Connor	Angela O'Donnell
Martin Sheen	Rose Pacatte
Jean Vanier	Michael W. Higgins
Dorothy Day	Patrick Jordan
Luis Antonio Tagle	Cindy Wooden
Georges and Pauline Vanier	Mary Francis Coady
Joseph Bernardin	Steven P. Millies
Corita Kent	Rose Pacatte
Daniel Rudd	Gary B. Agee
Helen Prejean	Joyce Duriga
Paul VI	Michael Collins
Thea Bowman	Maurice J. Nutt
Shahbaz Bhatti	John L. Allen Jr.
Rutilio Grande	Rhina Guidos
Elizabeth Johnson	Heidi Schlumpf
Augustus Tolton	Joyce Duriga
Paul Farmer	Jennie Weiss Block

More titles to follow . . .

Thea Bowman

Faithful and Free

Maurice J. Nutt

LITURGICAL PRESS
Collegeville, Minnesota

www.litpress.org

Cover design by Red+Company. Cover illustration by Philip Bannister.

Excerpts from *Thea's Song: The Life of Thea Bowman*, by Charlene Smith and John Feister, © 2009. Reprinted by permission of Orbis Books.

2   3   4   5   6   7   8   9

Library of Congress Control Number: 2018958562

ISBN 978-0-8146-4608-3   978-0-8146-4632-8 (e-book)

In loving memory of my parents and my brother:
Haller Levi and Beatrice Lucille Duvall Nutt
Haller Edward Nutt

By blood and by love I am bound to them, though I cannot look into their eyes or hear their voices. I honor their faith and faithfulness, their memory and history. I cherish their lives. I will tell their story, call their names, and thus keep them alive.

Contents

Acknowledgments

I acknowledge with great esteem and gratitude my friends Sister Charlene Smith, FSPA, and John Feister for their seminal work *Thea's Song: The Life of Thea Bowman* that I relied upon for guidance as I wrote this book. The inimitable Sister Thea came "back to life" through my insightful and engaging interviews with Sister Dorothy Ann "Dort" Kundinger, FSPA, Flonzie Brown-Wright, Mary Queen Donnelly, Cornelia Johnson, Doris O'Leary, Veronica Downs-Dorsey, Father Glenn D. Parker, CSsR, Father Manuel Williams, CR, and Sister Eva Marie Lumas, SSS. To Rocco Palmo, Father Bruce Neili, CSP, Dr. Brian L. Turner, Dr. Marcus S. Cox, Loretta Deville, Bernadette Cheri, Carolyn Duvigneaud Thomas, and Will Jemison—thank you for encouraging me to make "Thea known for a new generation." I continue to owe a debt of gratitude to my Redemptorist confreres of the Denver Province for your unwavering support of me. To Bishop Joseph R. Kopacz, PhD, bishop of the Diocese of Jackson in Mississippi, for believing in the sanctity of Thea Bowman and wanting to lift her up as a model to the world of prophetic holiness, missionary discipleship, and racial reconciliation by opening her cause for canonization. Likewise, I appreciate you entrusting me with assisting in Thea's cause for canonization.

To my family and dear friends: most especially my brothers Cordell and Michael Nutt, and Verona A. Bowers, Stephen and Helene LaBerta, Richard and Larissa Banks, Michael P. McMillan, Dr. Reginald K. Ellis, and Paul and Shirley Foster for your unconditional love and for always "being there" whenever I needed you. Above all, I express my appreciation to Barry Hudock for inviting me to write a biography of Thea Bowman for the People of God series; and to the staff at Liturgical Press for your patience and perseverance with me as "Thea and I wrestled" to make sure that *her* story was told the way *she* wanted it told.

Introduction

"I still didn't hear Mike Wallace say, 'Black is beautiful.'"
Confidently, albeit coerced, the veteran CBS News corre-
spondent responded to the Mississippi-born, black Catholic
sister's persuasion by repeating, "Black is beautiful!" And
the sister shouted with enthusiastic approval, "Amen!"

This is how many Americans were introduced to the charismatic and enthralling black,[1] vowed religious woman,
Sister Thea Bowman, FSPA. At every moment of the *60
Minutes* interview, Sister Thea was confident, poised, assured, direct, and well informed. When she felt like she
needed to, she threw a question back to Wallace, "What do
you think?" And though Wallace was telling *her* story, at all
times Sister Thea controlled *her* narrative. Sister Thea pos-
sessed what black "church folk" call "holy boldness," meaning that you speak your truth knowing that it comes from
the Lord. To minimize Sister Thea's "holy boldness" and
confidence as being any kind of self-aggrandizement would
be to miss the totality of her personality, her spirituality, her
mission, and her ministry. Thea was unapologetically simply
being Thea.

The *60 Minutes* segment featuring Sister Thea that aired
on May 3, 1987, held before the nation a black woman, an

1

engaging educator, an astute intellectual, an ardent advocate for racial justice and reconciliation; a soul stirring singer of the spiritual songs of her ancestors, a prophetic preacher, and an unconventional, African robe-wearing Catholic Sister. This mesmerizing televised interview featured a cancer-ridden sister who spread Gospel joy, brought healing to conflicts within communities and within the church, offered clarity to those who lacked understanding of the black Catholic experience, and taught us how to accept God's will while struggling, suffering, and ultimately dying. In her, we found someone extraordinary. Franciscan Sister of Perpetual Adoration Sister Thea Bowman was like no other person—and certainly no other nun—you would ever meet!

Well, no one ever "met" Thea; no, you *encountered* her. Her bodacious, engaging personality drew you to her. Once you had a "Thea encounter," you would never forget her. Her personality and joy were so infectious that her presence seems to remain with us still. When her friends speak of Sister Thea, it is difficult to speak of her in the past tense.

My first Thea encounter occurred in July of 1984. I was a professed Redemptorist seminarian attending my first Joint Conference of black Catholic clergy, permanent deacons and their wives, religious men and women, and seminarians. The meeting was held in New Orleans, and I was a bit shell-shocked at seeing so many black religious women and men. I had attended a mostly white seminary and was not used to being around so many people who looked like me and who shared the same vocation. The highlight of that year's Joint Conference was attending the very first commencement of the Institute for Black Catholic Studies (IBCS) at Xavier University of Louisiana, the only historically black and Catholic university in the nation. The three graduates—Sister Eva Marie Lumas, SSS, Sister Addie Lorraine Walker,

SSND, and Father James Voelker—would receive their master of theology (ThM) degrees in Black Catholic Studies, the first time such a degree was awarded in the nation's history. While I was elated to witness history, I was captivated by the speech given by the commencement speaker, Sister Thea Bowman, FSPA, PhD. It was the first time I had ever heard her speak, and I do not remember what she exactly said that evening. But I have never forgotten how she made me feel. Her words penetrated the very core of my emotions, especially my feelings about having to assimilate into the dominant culture of my religious community to be accepted. She validated my cultural heritage and religious expressions and encouraged me to share my gifts with the Catholic Church. I recall feeling embarrassed because I cried throughout Thea's commencement address. Indeed, it was a cathartic moment for me. It was for me a moment of spiritual and cultural emancipation and liberation to be the black and Catholic child of God I was created to be.

After the commencement ceremony, my Redemptorist confrere, Glenn Parker, CSsR, introduced me to his good friend, Sister Thea. I was so in awe of her that I remember simply saying hello and that she said how happy she was that the Redemptorists were getting more black vocations. My Redemptorist confrere encouraged me to join him at the IBCS and I enrolled the following summer in the master's degree program there.

I came to know Thea Bowman during the last six years of her life. While I didn't know it at the time, I met her the same year that she was diagnosed with breast cancer and the year that both her parents died. One can only imagine what a dreadful year 1984 must have been for her, and yet she carried on with her life and her teaching, preaching, singing, evangelizing, and spreading the joy of Jesus Christ with steadfast vigor and determination. Later I would learn that Thea's daily mantra throughout her struggle with cancer was that she was going to "live until she died." And that she did. As her student, I was amazed at her boundless energy as she taught her classes. Not knowing how long Sister Thea would live, I was committed to taking every class that she offered. I would also be the last student she would advise in the writing of their master's thesis. Without question, Thea Bowman was a demanding teacher. She could easily discern her students' cognitive and analytical abilities and would push them to produce their very best. If she thought that a student was not well prepared for a class presentation, she had no problem asking the student to sit down and come back to class better prepared tomorrow. She would not allow a student to present less than their best understanding of the material. Besides, Sister Thea was not going to let anyone waste her time or the class time by being unprepared! Seemingly tough as a classroom teacher, Sister Thea knew that she was not only preparing her students for classroom lessons but for life. She knew from her own lived experiences that nothing would be easily given to black students, and so they had to strive to be exceptional inside and outside of the classroom. Those were life-lessons that I am sure every student taught by Sister Thea Bowman has committed to memory and cherished in his or her heart.

The Thea Bowman story, like the woman herself, is far from banal or mundane. No, it is multifaceted, inspiring, and unconventional. Imagine growing up in the paradox of being the granddaughter of a former slave yet the only daughter and pride and joy of a middle-class educator and a physician amid the racism and segregation of the so-called separate but equal "Jim Crow" legal system of Mississippi. Her conversion to Catholicism was rooted in a pragmatic living of the Gospel of Jesus Christ as she witnessed and benefitted from the dedicated Franciscan Sisters of Perpetual Adoration who taught at her childhood school, Holy Child Jesus in Canton, Mississippi. Seeing faith in action in her hometown as a child undoubtedly shaped Thea's understanding of Christian discipleship. She also desired to witness to Jesus Christ by serving the poor and marginalized, by educating those who did not have equal access to adequate education, to give comfort to those who were oppressed by the unjust and the unreasonable laws of the land. The indelible mark and profound impression that these white Northern nuns made on this highly impressionable black Southern girl convinced her that God was indeed calling her to leave all the things that were familiar to her. The yearning to serve God was undeniable. In Canton, Mississippi this young girl gave up her birth name, Bertha, and became Sister Mary Thea. She left behind all things Southern, soulful, satisfying, and familiar to sojourn to a far-away northern town called La Crosse, Wisconsin, to things unfamiliar and not always satisfying—especially the food! Her commitment to her vows and to the religious way of life is summed up in one of the spirituals she loved to sing: *"Done made my vow to Lord, and I never will turn back. I will go, I shall go, to see what the end will be!"*[2]

That initial "yes" to God and the grace of perseverance was the beginning of a short but phenomenal life. Given the magnitude of the impact and outreach that this one woman had on the life of the Catholic Church in America and beyond, it is difficult to limit her vocation to one singular aspect. But Thea herself, when once asked what she understood her vocation to be about, assuredly answered, "I'm a teacher." I would have to concur, but with an understanding of the vocation of teacher in the broadest sense. She explained, "When I say education, I mean academic education, fiscal education, vocational education, parenting education, moral and value education, cultural education. We need a total educational package, and we need to make it available to everybody. And it's your responsibility, it's my responsibility. How can we impact the country in such a way that we can get a clear message to our elected leadership that this is what must be?"[3] Thea understood her vocation as a teacher in the holistic sense that no human person should be without equal opportunities to be fully functioning in society and in the church. She had a clear demand that "each one, teach one!" It was not a clever rhyme or a pious phrase, but an urgent admonition to take what you know or what you have learned and share it with others. Thea felt that it is only when we share our knowledge, our experiences, our perceived understanding, our customs and traditions, our stories, and our faith that we truly become all that we are called to be in humanity as well as in the church—to truly *be* the Body of Christ.

While Sister Thea is often lauded as a powerful preacher, an effective evangelizer, and a dynamic singer, yet in all those endeavors she was teaching us. You never left Sister Thea's presence without having learned something, experienced something, gained a new insight, garnered a new concept, gleaned a new possibility, or just felt like something had just happened to you simply by being in her company. And even if you couldn't figure it out at that very moment, you knew that somehow you were blessed by the encounter. That's what I mean about Thea being the consummate teacher. You were learning from her even when you didn't realize you were being taught.

While there are numerous Thea teachable moments, in my humble estimation there are two instances that are quite remarkable. I will elaborate on them in more detail in the telling of Thea's story, but they are also worth mentioning here.

The first remarkable lesson that Thea taught was when she was invited to address the United States bishops' conference at their June 1989 meeting at Seton Hall University. Thea wasn't feeling well, having undergone chemotherapy treatments for the vicious cancer that ravaged her body, most especially her bones. Wheeled to the center of the stage in her wheelchair, Thea spoke to the bishops as a sister having a "heart-to-heart" conversation with her brothers. She had something very important to say to them, something that needed to be said. While I will discuss later in detail what she said, it is important to note here the "Thea effect," the effect she had on people, her ability to take a very difficult and complex situation and through her innate genius and holiness speak in a way that diffused tension, anxiety, and fear and ushered in understanding, peace, reconciliation, and even renewal and reparation. Make no mistake about it: class was in session and Sister Dr. Thea Bowman, FSPA, even in her sickness and fragility delivered an unforgettable, well-crafted, and—in her typical Thea folksy fashion—spontaneous message on the struggle for racial justice and the need for evangelization, Catholic education, and full participation and inclusivity for black Catholics in the Roman Catholic Church in America. In a word, Thea was masterful.

Secondly, Thea exemplified in a very clear and conscious way what it means to accept suffering and death. During her six-year journey with cancer, she prayed for God's healing. Her faith enabled her to truly believe that if God didn't give her what she asked for, then God would give her something better. Because of her closeness to many people, Thea permitted her friends, colleagues, and students to visit her at her family home in Canton as she neared death. She welcomed their prayers, story-telling, fond remembrances, laugher, singing, and sometimes simply their quiet presence in the room when she drifted off to sleep. In her final days on this side of "the river Jordan," the teacher, evangelist, television personality, songstress, and prophetic preacher who had commanded audiences globally in classrooms, cathedrals, concert halls, and front porches did not want to be alone as she waited on the Lord to call her home. This "old folks' child" had packed more life and living in her fifty-two years than most would or could have in a century. So she, deservedly, peacefully passed away at her family home at 136 Hill Street in Canton, Mississippi, but she didn't die alone.

Throughout her life, Thea was so ubiquitous on the Catholic scene that it seems strange that there is now a generation who never knew her. There is an African proverb that contends that if you say the name of a loved one who has passed on, they will never die. Thea Bowman's life and legacy lives on in the names, images, and ministries of many schools (parochial and public), institutions, religious education programs, halls, foundations, scholarships, liturgical Mass settings, gospel choirs, healthcare centers, women's shelters, youth ministry centers, social service ministries, prayer rooms, stained glass windows, holy cards, paintings, sculptures, statues, and books (and now this book you are now holding in your hand), but more importantly for those of us who knew and loved and cherished her in our hearts, in those who are coming to know her and seek her intercession. I'm fairly confident that our beloved Sister Thea will be remembered for a very long time.

CHAPTER ONE

Being Bertha Bowman
(1937–1953)

I'm what they used to call an "old folks' child."
When I was growing up, my parents, especially my
mother, made a concerted effort to keep me in touch
with the elders. She wanted me to hear from them.
She wanted me to learn the old songs and the old
stories. She wanted me to learn from their lips about
slavery and what they had been through.[1]

Sister Thea Bowman, FSPA

Mississippi, like other Southern States in America, is
tainted by its horrid history of slavery. Slavery is one of the
world's worst mass atrocities. Twelve million Africans were
kidnapped, enslaved, and shipped across the Atlantic to the
Americas under horrific conditions. The brutal and inhu-
mane treatment of enslaved Africans who were brought to
the shores of the United States was like none other seen in
the world. Africans captured from West Africa were packed
and chained together like sardines in the bottom of slave
ships for months, barely surviving the long transatlantic

journey. Nearly two million of them died at sea during the agonizing journey. Barely given nourishment, they endured diseases, torture, and the treacherous weather conditions while at sea. Once in America, these enslaved Africans were separated from all that was familiar to them: geographic locations, tribes, languages and dialects, customs and religions. They were also separated from one another to ensure that they could not communicate and thus not revolt against their sadistic treatment. The slave trade in America equipped plantation owners with the forced human labor to maintain their cotton, rice, and tobacco crops and their vast households. For centuries, enslaved Africans were held in bondage and randomly sold and separated without any regard to family ties or intimate relationships. They were verbally, physically, psychologically, and sexually abused and humiliated. If they dared to escape and were caught, they were brutally punished, maimed, or killed. Being an enslaved African in America meant that they were property and less than human, with no rights, respect, or recourse.

Slaveholders employed ministers who, using the Scriptures to justify slavery, instructed slaves to be obedient, respectful, and always to maintain a disposition of servitude. Enslaved Africans had a profound understanding of God and had their own rituals and belief systems, as well as their devotions and forms of worship. In fact, it was these secret, clandestine moments of communing with the Divine that spiritually and psychologically sustained the enslaved Africans amid the brutality of slavery. Whenever possible, slaves went deep in the woods, far away from their plantations, to what they referred to you as "hush harbors" to secretly pray and worship free from the restrictions placed on them while in the presence of their slaveholders or overseers. These religious gatherings happened after dark when their field and house work was finished and they could move away from the plantation without being noticed. Coded announcements of these secret meetings could be spread to enslaved Africans through song. For example, someone might sing "Go Down Moses" or "Steal Away" as a signal that it was "hush harbor" time. The overseer would think that the person was simply singing a spiritual song, unaware that the slaves were moving far into the bush to meet with God. The "hush harbor" served as a location where the slaves could combine their African religious traditions with Christianity. According to Rice University's religious studies professor Anthony B. Pinn, "In these secret services, slaves would preach a different version of the gospel, one that highlighted God's desire that they be freed. These sermons were also laced with calls for justice and righteousness, and with a critique of slaveholders who claimed to be Christians yet treated other humans—Africans—as less than human. How was this consistent with the gospel's call for love?"[2] The "hush harbor" service involved sacred dance, hand clapping, and holy shouts unto God in praise, lament, anguish, and seeking liberation. It was here, too, where the Negro spiritual originated, whereby enslaved Africans would reinterpret stories from the Bible that had double meaning, revealing ideas of religious salvation and freedom from slavery. They especially identified with the stories of the children of Israel and understood themselves, like the Jews, to be the chosen of God who would one day experience freedom.[3] Through their enslavement, the Africans understood the core of Christianity to be that the Son of God named Jesus had suffered, died, and rose again to set the world free. It was this spiritual and earthly freedom that they, too, desired. Not knowing for certain when the opportunity for another "hush harbor" meeting would come, they took advantage of this precious time with God and the meeting would last late into the evening.

Even after the Emancipation Proclamation decree[4] and the ratification of the Thirteenth Amendment of the US Constitution, which abolished slavery and involuntary servitude except as punishment for a crime, Africans now living in America were not truly free because they had little to no economic, social, or political power to sustain and advance them. Many Africans in the South remained on plantations and continued to care for their former slave owners, while others sharecropped, meaning having to pay and or give produce to their former slave owners to work the land they formerly worked as slaves. Injustice and inequality was the oppressive lot of the children of Africa, and many remained servile to those who had held them in bondage.

Seventy-two years after slavery ended and the struggle for racial justice and equality continued, in Yazoo City, Mississippi, on Wednesday, December 29, 1937, a baby girl was born from the union of Dr. Theon Bowman and Mary Esther Coleman Bowman. They considered naming their newborn daughter Rosemarie. But that was not to be. Dr. and Mrs. Bowman would give their one and only child the name of a beloved relative. The baby girl was named Bertha after her father's younger sibling and only sister. Aunt Bertha insisted that Theon and Mary Esther give their newborn daughter her name. Bertha Bowman never had children and this new member of the Bowman family bearing her name would certainly be a precious gift to her. This newborn child was born into an ancestral lineage like most African American families and yet this family was unique in its spirit of compassion, striving toward achievement, seeking further knowledge through education, deep and abiding dependence on God, and unwavering commitment of service to others. These noble characteristics would be manifested in the life and witness of Theon and Mary Esther's newborn daughter.

Theon Edward Bowman had been born on September 13, 1894, in Yazoo City, where his parents, Edward and Sallie Bowman, had established their home. The Bowmans were Methodists. Theon was the firstborn of three children. He had two younger siblings: his sister Bertha Catherine Bowman, born in 1899, who never married and lived most of her life in Memphis, and a brother, Jemison Charles Bowman, born in 1900, who would become a pharmacist and neighborhood drugstore owner on Memphis's southside.

Theon Bowman received his elementary and high school education in the Memphis public school system. He completed his college education in Nashville. He earned his medical degree from Nashville's Meharry Medical School in 1918, one of the few medical schools in the country that African Americans could attend. As a distinguished gentleman and scholar, the newly minted Dr. Bowman was eventually initiated into the Alpha Phi Alpha Fraternity, the first black collegiate fraternity founded on the campus of Cornell University, in Ithaca, New York, in 1906.[5] Theon journeyed north to New York for his medical residency. He decided to practice medicine in Canton, Mississippi, because the black community there had no black doctors to care for them. Dr. Bowman established his office within walking distance of the Bowman home at 136 Hill Street. This town would be where he would practice medicine for over fifty years, raise his family, and be a pillar in the community for the rest of his life.

Mary Esther Coleman Bowman, born November 25, 1902, had a formidable lineage in Greenville, Mississippi, in the Mississippi Delta. Her parents were Jerry and Lizzie Williams Coleman. Lizzie was a highly acclaimed educator in Greenville. She taught public school for forty-seven years and was principal of the largest African American public elementary school in Greenville. A high school in Greenville was renamed as the Lizzie Coleman Public School in 1923 by the local school board in recognition for her dedication to educating African American youth.[6]

It is no wonder that Thea would one day become an outstanding teacher. Education was in her familial DNA. Her mother, Mary Esther Coleman, graduated from Tougaloo College, north of Jackson, Mississippi, in 1919. Afterward, Mary Esther went to Chicago to attend summer school classes at Chicago Normal College.[7] She returned to her hometown of Greenville and like her mother Lizzie, she began working as a schoolteacher.

Eight years her senior, tall, debonair, Dr. Theon Bowman met his future bride, Mary Esther Coleman, at the home of her aunt in Yazoo City. The couple were smitten and dated for six months before Dr. Bowman proposed to the Greenville schoolteacher on Christmas Eve, 1924.[8] The wedding was set for 1925. The ceremony did not take place in a church building, probably because Theon and Mary Esther did not share the same denomination; Dr. Bowman was Methodist and Miss Coleman was Episcopalian. Instead the wedding was held on the lawn of the Coleman home in Greenville. Some fifty guests sat on lawn chairs and the wedding ceremony was officiated by an Episcopal priest, Reverend S. A. Morgan, and assisted by a Methodist minister, Rev. J. R. Rowe.[9]

By 1937, Theon was forty-three years old and Mary Esther was thirty-five years old. For the era, Mrs. Bowman was considered too old to be a first-time mother. Thea would later describe herself as an "old folks' child" due to her parents' advanced ages. Dr. Bowman was elated that his beloved Mary Esther was soon to give birth to their child, and yet he was extremely cautious as the anticipated December birth date grew closer. He drove his beloved wife to Yazoo City to be cared for by her good friend and registered nurse Miss Alice Luse. He also wanted his wife to be in Yazoo City because Canton did not have a hospital for African Americans. The Bowman's child would be delivered at Yazoo City's Old African Hospital.[10] Everyone was ready for the birth of the Bowman baby and had made careful preparations; all was in order, or at least they thought. Here's how Thea told the story of her birth:

> My mother, they tell me, went downtown Wednesday morning, December 29, the fifth day of Christmas, to make some last-minute purchases for the new baby. But she went into labor, and had to return home quickly as she could. Miss Alice Luse called my father at his doctor's office in Canton. He got into his car and immediately drove the forty-five miles to Yazoo City. Then Miss Alice called Dr. L. T. Miller.
> Dr. Miller said it was too soon. He took his time driving to the Luse home. By the time Dr. Miller arrived, my own father had delivered me! When Dr. Miller finally arrived, Miss Alice, having swaddled the brand new, perfect and beautiful, six-pound baby girl, answered the door with the child in her arms, just to prove that Dr. Miller wasn't always right.[11]

To celebrate the joyous birth of his beautiful baby daughter, Dr. Bowman bought a bottle of expensive French champagne. He bought the champagne not to drink and celebrate with his friends, but to be preserved for a toast one day at his daughter's wedding reception. The champagne was a 1928 vintage Heidsieck Brut from Reims, France. Of course, there would be no wedding reception and thus the thunderous popping of the cork never happened.[12]

Less than two months after baby Bertha Bowman's birth, her parents presented her for her christening at St. Mark's Episcopal Church in Jackson on February 13, 1938. Reverend Arthur Buxton Keeling, who was also Bertha's godfather, christened her Bertha Elizabeth Bowman.[13]

As Bertha spent her early days of childhood in the Bowman family home in Canton, Theon and Mary Esther sought to expose their young daughter to the gift of music. They taught her nursery rhymes, the alphabet, and how to count. Young Bertha was quite fond of her mother reading children's stories to her at bedtime and throughout the day. Bertha marveled at all there was to learn, and she was very eager to gain new knowledge. She was an inquisitive child. Her mother, being a teacher, did not wait for formal training at school; Mary Esther would teach her daughter all the essentials long before she ever entered a classroom.

Mary Esther, a genteel Southerner, had hopes that her beautiful young daughter would be prim, proper, and at all times a sophisticated little lady. Though she would dress Bertha in frilly, doll-like dresses and tie ribbons in her hair, Bertha's illuminating and outgoing personality was evident early. The future Sister Thea would often reminisce with her friends how at times as a child her dear mother found her incorrigible because she was not prim and proper but often boisterous and over-the-top. She mused that she had inherited Dr. Bowman's wit, humor, and fondness for practical jokes. Bertha especially liked to tease her father and anxiously awaited his return home from his medical office so she could tease and play with him and tell him all about her day.

The Bowmans nevertheless were doting parents, and Bertha, whom they nicknamed "Birdie," was at the center of their joy. To speak of her playfulness is not to say that young Bertha was unruly or disrespectful; quite the opposite. She was always respectful and well mannered, especially in the presence of the grown-ups and elders. Bertha was kind and wise beyond her years. Most certainly she witnessed the compassion and wisdom of her parents. Bertha was also an only child living with older parents, and so she was always in earshot of adult conversations. Naturally, she became used to mature topics of conversation and less childish banter.

Bertha's spiritual sensibilities were also evident as a young child. She enjoyed going to church with her friends as a child. Bertha was in awe of the music, preaching, and fellowship of her Protestant upbringing. Thea, recounting stories of her childhood and introduction to religion, would later remark that it was in those "old black churches that I learned what they called the 'old-time religion.' I wanted to grow up so I could be a preacher."[14]

Bertha began attending a public school in Canton at age three. At the same time, she also started going to Sunday school. She met with other neighborhood children in the home of their teacher, Mother Ricker, who taught them Bible stories, spirituals, and gospel music.[15] At a very early age, Bertha was learning what would eventually become her hallmark—bringing faith alive through preaching, teaching, singing, and praising.

It was during this period that Bertha met Mrs. Ward, a next-door neighbor whom she would, as an adult, refer to frequently in her preaching, teaching, and storytelling. Thea would paint a vivid picture of how Mrs. Ward, a domestic worker, would go work for the white folks during the week, wearing her maid's uniform, but appear quite different on Sunday morning, the Lord's Day. As with most church-going black folks, Sunday was the day that you dressed in your

Sunday best and you honored God by going to church looking your best and giving your best in worship. Thea would
dramatically detail how Mrs. Ward would "have church"
before going to church. She would wake up early singing
her jubilee, her song of praise, proclaiming the goodness of
Jesus throughout her house, on the porch, in her garden,
and then throughout the neighborhood as she made her way
to the Lord's house. For Mrs. Ward and so many of the elders around during Birdie Bowman's formative years, religion wasn't what you did only on Sunday morning; it was
a part of who you were. Bertha learned from the elders that
there was joy in serving the Lord and that joy permeated
one's whole being.

In a commentary that Thea would later write in a song-
book of spirituals, *Sister Thea: Songs of My People*, she
wrote, "I grew up in a community where the teaching of
religion was a treasured role of the elders—grandparents,
old uncles and aunts, but also parents, big brothers and
sisters, family, friends, and church members. Many of the
best teachers were not formally educated. But they knew
Scripture, and they believed the Living Word must be celebrated and shared."[16] While Bertha's early childhood de-
nominational affiliation was betwixt and between both the
Episcopalian and United Methodist churches, as well as other
Protestant denominations, she would say later in life that
there was something in the Catholic Church that captured
and kept her and that she didn't need to look anywhere else.

In 1941, a religious congregation of men called the Missionary Servants of the Most Holy Trinity (popularly known
as the Trinitarians) and an associated congregation for
women called the Missionary Servants of the Most Blessed
Trinity came to Canton to serve the white Catholics at Sacred Heart Catholic Mission. A few years later, after dia-

logue with the African American community who voiced a
desperate need for quality education for their children, the
Trinitarians established Holy Child Jesus Mission in 1946.
The Mission first opened a school and shortly afterward a
parish. Establishing a school and church in this small Mississippi town for the impoverished African American community seemed an insurmountable and arduous task,
considering both anti-Catholic and racist sentiments of
many local white people, as well as a scarcity of financial
resources. However, during this time and throughout the
years, the bishop of the Diocese of Natchez (now the Diocese of Jackson) was sympathetic to the pastoral and educational needs of the black community.[17]

Thea would later reflect that it was not necessarily the
teachings of the church or the liturgy that drew her at such
a young age to become Catholic; rather it was the personal
witness of the priests, sisters, and laity at Holy Child Jesus
that greatly influence her conversion. She saw their commitment to the poor and marginalized, their sense of community and prayerfulness, and their sincere care and concern
for one another and for others. Even as a young child, Bertha instinctively knew that "being church" was about wit-
nessing to the Gospel of Jesus Christ by being Christ to
others, especially to those who lacked hope or joy. In her
eagerness to join the Catholic faith, nine-year-old Bertha
was "conditionally"[18] baptized on Sunday, June 1, 1947, at
Holy Child Jesus Catholic Church at 315 Garrett Street by
the pastor, Father Justin Furman, a Trinitarian. Bertha made
her First Holy Communion the following day.[19]

Bertha's parents allowed their insightful and independent
young daughter decide to become Roman Catholic on her
own, while they remained at the time members of their own
respective denominations. Bertha's conversion to Catholicism

was so inspiring that this faith-filled child would lead her beloved parents into the Catholic faith several years later, first Mary Esther and then Theon. The Bowmans' conversion through the example of Bertha was clearly the embodiment of Isaiah 6:11: ". . . and a little child will lead them."

Bertha attended the local public school for black children in Canton from the first to the fifth grade. Dr. and Mrs. Bowman, knowing that their daughter was highly intelligent, insatiably curious, and ever inquisitive, were aware that she would no longer be challenged by the poor quality of education at Canton's "colored" public school. The state of Mississippi allocated unjust and unequal financial assistance to "colored" schools as opposed to white schools. Many public schools had outdated and used textbooks and unfit school buildings, and the academically qualified school-teachers who taught there did not receive salaries equal to those of their white counterparts. Bertha began her education in the Mississippi public schools in 1941, some thirteen years before the groundbreaking United States Supreme Court *Brown v. The Board of Education* decision in 1954. Bertha Bowman was not afforded the sort of quality education that would help her and her classmates thrive and succeed. Fortunately, her mother, an educator herself, refused to allow her gifted daughter to fall behind and continually reviewed her studies with her at home.

The saying "God writes straight with crooked lines" surely applies to the educational trajectory of young Bertha's life. As the Bowmans were looking for a better educational opportunity for their daughter, help was heading to Canton by way of the Franciscan Sisters of Perpetual Adoration (FSPA), a group of religious women who first came to America to educate German immigrants in the northwestern city of La Crosse, Wisconsin. After many letters sent to the

Mother Superior by the Trinitarian Missionaries, pleading with her to send sisters to educate the local impoverished black youth, as well as a personal visit from Father Lawrence to the motherhouse in La Crosse, the Franciscan Sisters of Perpetual Adoration relented and accepted the invitation to go to this place far from their Wisconsin base. A 1950 book on the history of the Franciscan Sisters of Perpetual Adoration, offers this account:

> Father Andrew Lawrence, ST, was preaching in the Midwest at the time (in 1942). He got himself invited to talk with the sisters at St. Rose Convent, pleading Father Hay's need for sisters to teach at the school. Both priests were persuasive. Father Lawrence began correspondence with the sisters. He frequently expressed hope that they would accept the challenge of starting a school in one of the southern communities he served. In 1946, Mother Rose Kreibich, FSPA, major superior (head of the community), visited Canton and, realizing the need, promised Father Lawrence that the sisters would help with one of the "most urgent needs of the mid-twentieth century."[20]

The same author noted the challenges as well as opportunities that the novice FSPA missionaries would encounter: "Once the FSPA had come to Canton and established the new school, they knew how important their role was, and they dedicated themselves to it without one look back. In every sense, the term 'mission' is applicable to Holy Child Jesus School. In Mississippi, where the colored make up one half of the total population of 2,200,000, Catholics number about forty-four thousand; of those forty-four thousand, fewer than five thousand are colored."[21]

African Americans constitute a clear majority of the population of Canton, around seventy-five percent of the over thirteen thousand residents of the city. The Catholic population of Canton was small. The city of Canton was indeed a ripe harvest for Catholic evangelization. While many African Americans in Canton belonged to Protestant denominations, there were more who did not attend church services on a regular basis or not at all. The Trinitarian Missionaries and the Franciscan Sisters of Perpetual Adoration had their work cut out for them. Before opening a school, the sisters had to spend time visiting homes and recruiting students to attend. Since the convent was established in the African American community, it was important that the sisters spent time getting to know and building relationships among their neighbors. Establishing a meaningful connection and building trust naturally took time. Neither the sisters nor the African American community knew much about one another. However, the black community desperately wanted quality education for their children and they were willing to entrust their children to these northern Catholic Sisters so that they would receive the best education possible.

Mary Esther Bowman expected much of her only child. Bertha would soon be old enough for high school and her reading was only at a third-grade level. The all-black public school in Canton was not preparing her adequately.[22] As soon as the announcement came that the new Catholic school was ready to open, the Bowmans wasted no time in moving their daughter there. Bertha would be a member of the charter sixth-grade class of Holy Child Jesus Catholic School, one of approximately ninety pupils enrolled in the school for the 1948–1949 school year.[23] Although the school building was an old Army barracks, the parents and students were less bothered by what the school looked like than they were grateful for the learning that would take place in the makeshift classrooms. This Catholic school helped Bertha advance in reading and learning. Years later, she would recall how this change in educational environments afforded her an opportunity to expand her learning and equipped her with the tools to succeed:

> Because my mother wanted me to have a chance in life, she sent me to a Catholic school. The black public schools were tremendously disadvantaged and understaffed. At the black Catholic school, I remember using books given to us by St. Angela's Academy in Carroll, Iowa, and Aquinas High School in La Crosse, Wis.
>
> We shared gym clothes with students in Breda, Iowa. The sisters begged a lot, and because they did, our school was much better supplied. Men and women all over the country gave a dollar or two to help us get an adequate education.
>
> The priests, brothers, and sisters brought an extraordinary kind of dedication to the education process. They involved us in fundraising and helped us to educate ourselves. That was the key. They also worked with our parents and never left us feeling indebted. They made us feel that we contributed to the process.[24]

Like so many Catholic missionaries who went to the South in the 1940s and '50s to help assist black people amid the tumultuous upheaval of racism and inequality, the Franciscan Sisters of Perpetual Adoration came to Canton sincerely seeking to help, and the students invited to Holy Child Jesus School were welcomed regardless of race, religion, or economic status. The future Sister Thea would later reflect:

> The vast majority of the students were Baptist, Methodist, and Holiness. There were at most two dozen Catholics in a student population of 180. Holy Child was a good place to be.

We loved our teachers because they first loved us. For a handful, of Catholics, for devout Protestants, for the children of a surprising number of ministers, deacons, elders, and evangelizers, and for children who rarely went to any church, the Catholic school was a graced and grace-filled environment. We all went to Mass each week, sang in the choir, learned, if we wished, to serve Mass (boys only) or to care for vestments and altar (girls only). We all prayed before each class. We all studied catechism. With Father Gilbert [Hay] and Father Justin [Furman], religion class was a time to be anticipated and treasured—stories of Jesus and the saints, songs, and prayers, and Catholic doctrine. Our pastors loved us. They entertained us as they taught us. Some of my friends and schoolmates developed insights and skills (reading, thought, judgment, song), which enabled them to become young leaders in the Protestant churches in Canton.[25]

Sister Thea was keenly aware of the conglomeration of children who comprised the student body of her elementary school as she recalled in a fundraising newsletter regarding her experiences as a child attending Holy Child Jesus School: "What an amalgam of children we were—some hungry; some afraid; some eager and inquisitive; some shy; far too behind ever to catch up academically; some far too old, even for sixth grade; most already discouraged with school and learning; some too poor to pay even the $2 per month tuition that was asked but not required."[26]

The vital ministry of the Sisters at Holy Child Jesus School made a profound impact on the lives of the children of Canton. They received a challenging education that brought them to their grade-appropriate level of learning and were instilled with the desire to learn and achieve, as well as tenets of good citizenship, discipline, and Christian discipleship.

Students were assigned homework each day and were expected to have it completed. The students were proud of their school and did their part of make sure that the classrooms were clean and orderly.

The sisters who came to Canton were also concerned about the social well being of the black community. The sisters organized classes to teach nutrition and first aid to the impoverished community. They sought to help young pregnant women care for themselves during their pregnancy. They also organized a used clothing store known as the "sale house" or the "HCJ Emporium" and solicited donations to stock it from across the country. [27] This store was very important to the local community because struggling families and individuals could afford high quality clothes at bargain prices. The neat and fashionable clothing gave their new owners a sense of dignity and respect. The sisters were learning that sometimes the simplest thing, such as owning a pretty dress or a striking suit, would make an incredible difference in the lives of the black community.

While Bertha was attending Cameron Street public school, she had befriended a dear and lifelong friend, Doris Jones (later Doris O'Leary). Bertha was three years younger than Doris, but because she was an "old folks' child," she often had more in common with older children. Doris and Bertha became fast friends and enjoyed playing together, reading books, and singing songs. Dr. and Mrs. Bowman knew that being an only child was at times lonely for their daughter. When Bertha was eight years old and Doris was eleven, the Bowmans asked Doris's father if Doris could come and live in their home as a playmate for their daughter Bertha. Doris's mother had passed away some years earlier and as a widower left to care for his children by himself, he didn't mind Doris going to live in the Bowman household. Doris O'Leary later recalled, "Living with the Bowman family was very special. [Bertha] was like a sister to me and the Dr. and Mrs. Bowman treated me like I was their daughter. [Bertha] had two twin beds in her room that I shared with her. She had lots of toys but most of all she loved to read and had her own library in her room as a child. I never saw so many books in someone's home!"[28] When Doris moved in with the Bowmans, she too, transferred from public school and the Bowmans enrolled and paid for her to attend Holy Child Jesus School along with their daughter. Doris was not Catholic at the time but quickly converted as a child. She reflected, "The Franciscan Sisters were so nice to us, you just knew that they really cared for us. The sisters oversaw the Girl Scout troop. I became a Girl Scout and shortly after that I started going to catechism classes because of the fine example of the sisters. I was happy to become a Catholic." At home in the evenings, after she and Bertha finished their homework, they would go to their room and pray the rosary. "[Bertha] taught me how to pray the rosary," Doris remembered.[29]

Doris O'Leary fondly remembers how Bertha loved to spend her free time as a child helping other children or assisting adults in need. She entertained herself as well as the other children by either reading or singing to them and putting on plays. "[Bertha] had a wonderful sense of humor and loved singing, dancing, and acting."[30]

Besides both her prayerfulness and her playfulness, Doris recalled two other notable characteristics about young Bertha. "She was very smart; she enjoyed school and loved learning. [And] Bertha was the most generous person that I had ever met. Often, a fellow classmate who didn't have any food for lunch or who was still hungry, Bertha would quickly offer the student her lunch and would go without." Doris remembers that when she asked Bertha why she would

give away her lunch, "she would give me her big contagious
smile and say, 'That's okay, I'll be alright, and besides they
needed my lunch more than I did.'"[31] Eventually, Bertha
had her mother making brown paper bag lunches filled with
peanut butter and jelly sandwiches and other goodies for
the children in the school who didn't have anything to eat.
Bertha also convinced her mother to sew uniforms for the
children whose parents could not afford to buy school uniforms. Bertha made sure that her mother completed the
uniforms with the distinctive "HCJ" insignia.

Bertha loved spending time with the Franciscan Sisters.
She and her good friend Flonzie Brown sought opportunities to visit the convent, and the sisters enjoyed their fre-
quent visits. The seed of a religious vocation was planted
very early in Bertha's life, and she carefully nurtured it
through prayer and by emulating the lives and practices of
these Sisters from La Crosse. Bertha would "play nun" by
putting a scarf on her head and pretending it was the veil
of a religious habit, even when she would visit the convent,
all to the amusement and encouragement of the Sisters.[32]
Bertha would often pray her rosary as the sisters prayed
theirs, strolling the grounds of the Holy Child Jesus Mission.
It was evident to the Franciscan Sisters of Perpetual Adoration, Bertha's childhood friends, fellow church members,
and those in the community that "Birdie" would one day
become a vowed religious sister. When Bertha was fourteen
years old, she convinced Flonzie, then eleven, that they
would both one day go to the convent and become Franciscan Sisters. But Bertha had failed to realize that her beloved
friend Flonzie was not Catholic. Indeed, her family were
longtime members of the local Church of God congregation. Decades later, Flonzie recalled gleefully telling her
mother that she was going to be a Catholic nun, and her

mother without missing a beat responded, "Baby, I don't think that's going to happen."[33] To say that her teachers, the good Catholic sisters from the north, enthralled Bertha would indubitably be an understatement.

Everyone else may have been convinced that Bertha would one day become a sister, but her parents were not. Not only did Dr. and Mrs. Bowman—the former then a Methodist and the latter then Episcopalian—not approve of their daughter considering the Catholic sisterhood, they outright objected. Naturally, the Bowmans had other dreams for their bright and outgoing daughter. Besides, they had hoped to have grandchildren. There were many long and difficult discussions with their teenage daughter about her perceived religious vocation. When Bertha's parents ultimately forbade her to leave Canton to go to St. Rose High School located nine hundred miles away, at the motherhouse of the Franciscan Sisters of Perpetual Adoration in La Crosse, Wisconsin, they thought that was the end of the discussion.

In response, Bertha, ever determined to pursue her vocation, refused to eat. Doris O'Leary vividly recalls what she deemed her "hunger strike in order to go to the convent": "She wouldn't eat a thing and became so thin. Her poor parents were so troubled by her refusal to eat that they agreed to let her go to the convent."[34] One can only imagine fifteen-year-old Bertha's elation when her parents gave her their permission and somewhat reluctantly their blessing to travel so far away from home to answer her call.

CHAPTER TWO

Becoming Sister Thea Bowman, FSPA (1953–1961)

> I see my role as a sister, as a Franciscan Sister of Perpetual Adoration, as the role of every Christian—to share the Good News of the Lord Jesus Christ, to be Church.[1]
>
> Sister Thea Bowman, FSPA

While giving his only daughter permission to enter the Franciscan Sisters of Perpetual Adoration's high school in La Crosse, the wise and pragmatic Dr. Bowman also sternly cautioned his young and perhaps naïve, southern-born-and-bred offspring that she was traveling to uncharted territory: "They're not going to like you up there, the only black in the middle of all the whites." Bertha's response was, "I'm going to *make* them like me."[2]

Bertha would not have to journey alone to La Crosse. The Franciscan Sisters' leadership arranged for a sister, Lina Putz, FSPA, who taught at St. Rose High School to go to Canton and accompany Bertha to Wisconsin. Bertha already knew her, because she had previously spent a summer at

Holy Child Jesus in Canton. Given the laws of racial segregation in the South in 1953, the train trip out of Mississippi
would present some inevitable complications. Blacks were
not allowed to travel with whites in the same passenger cars.
But quite remarkably, the sisters negotiated with train of-
ficials to allow Bertha to ride with Sister Lina in the "whites
only" passenger section. The presence of a strikingly attrac-
tive, tall, lean, black teenage girl sitting next to a habit-clad
white sister in the all-white passenger car must have been
an interesting and intriguing sight for the passengers, and
perhaps a disturbing one for some. But Bertha paid them
no mind, because she was on a journey to pursue her God-
ordained vocation. The train stopped in Chicago, where
they had a layover and shared the hospitality of the Notre
Dame sisters' convent there. Then Sister Lina and the young
Canton student boarded a train from Chicago to La Crosse
and came to the end of their northward sojourn in La Crosse
on August 21, 1953.

La Crosse, a city nestled on Wisconsin's western border,
was much larger than Bertha's native Canton. While her
beloved Canton had a majority black population, in this
Wisconsin town very few black families were to be found.
Undoubtedly, the ever-inquisitive "Birdie" had researched
everything germane to where she would be living and was
prepared to survive and perhaps thrive in this "foreign land."

It was customary for all new entrants coming to the
motherhouse of the Franciscan Sisters of Perpetual Adoration
to make an initial visit to the beautiful and awe-inspiring
Maria Angelorum Chapel, where sisters were constantly
present in adoration prayer before the Blessed Sacrament.
Young Bertha was no exception to this rule. Upon entering
the chapel, Bertha felt a sense of peace; she knew in her heart
that she had made the right decision and received confirma-

tion that this was indeed her new home. After her visit, Bertha went directly to the aspirants' dormitory and changed into the mandatory attire of a simple black dress for aspirants. A sheer black chapel veil would be given to her later to be worn when in chapel.[3]

Bertha's arrival at St. Rose Convent was no secret in La Crosse. In fact, her presence quickly made news among the townspeople. The *La Crosse Catholic Register*, the diocesan newspaper, reported on the first black aspiring sister to enter the convent in La Crosse. The news story featured a photo of Bertha saying farewell to her parents and several Franciscan sisters in front of Holy Child Mission in Canton, with the bold heading, "Negro Aspirant." The caption under the photo read, "Bertha E. Bowman, aspirant for St. Rose's Convent, La Crosse, bids farewell to her parents, Dr. and Mrs. T.E. Bowman, Canton, Miss. Bertha, a junior in high school and a convert, is the first girl to enter the St. Rose aspirancy from the Holy Child Jesus Mission conducted for the Colored in Canton by the La Crosse Franciscans."[4]

Bertha from an early age nurtured a love for words and developed an expansive vocabulary. Words and their meanings fascinated her. The budding logophile honed her appreciation for letter-writing while at St. Rose Convent. Telephone conversations in the convent were extremely rare and the young aspirants were encouraged to send letters home to their families. The loquacious daughter of a physician and educator basked in writing letters home to her family and friends. Since she could not speak to her parents on the telephone, she used her writing talents to regale them. The letters contained stories about her new life in the convent, the daily occurrences of community life, the Wisconsin weather (most especially the winter season with its continuous snowfalls), her studies, and the new friends she made in religious life. Her vivid letters portrayed the somewhat mundane daily life of a religious convent as an adventure.

Convent life could certainly be a different sort of life for a teenage girl. But Bertha knew what the demands and rigor of living the life of a religious aspirant would entail. The Franciscan sisters back home in Canton had prepared her well. For the most part, adjusting to her new way of life was not very difficult for Bertha. She was resolved to do her best to live out the dictates required to become a Franciscan Sister of Perpetual Adoration. She knew that everything had its purpose, and even if she didn't like something she was resigned to it and never complained. There were a few things that required some adjustments. The future Sister Thea, while excited to see her first snowfall, found the brutal Wisconsin winters challenging, and she missed the typically warm seasons of the year in her beloved South. Bertha also missed her mother's home-cooked meals. The food served in the convent was mostly from Germanic and Irish cultural cuisines. She probably never became accustomed to or enjoyed the unfamiliar fare she was served, but she ate the fodder for the sake of sustenance. One thing is for sure: the convent food was bland and lacked the southern seasoning so familiar to Bertha.

Academically, Bertha stood out among her fellow aspirants as a scholar. Bertha simply loved learning and excelled in most of her studies. Although never acknowledged by her religious superiors, there was an expectation that as a "Negro aspirant" Bertha had to be exceptional to persevere. The La Crosse Franciscans in Canton knew that she was extremely bright and deserving of entrance into their religious community. However, Bertha knew that she would once again have to prove her worthiness to the sisters at St. Rose Convent. Bertha was mindful that she not only had to "make due" or "fit in"; as a black young woman, she also had to exceed all expectations. She would later recall, "If I was cold [in the convent] I would just be cold. If I was hungry, I would just be hungry."[5]

Bertha was confident that she belonged in the convent, but some of the sisters responsible for her religious formation perhaps initially questioned why she was there. Most young, black Catholic women interested in a religious vocation were limited to considering the three communities of black women, namely, the Oblate Sisters of Providence founded by Servant of God Mother Mary Lange in Baltimore in 1829; the Sisters of the Holy Family founded by Venerable Mother Henriette DeLille in New Orleans in 1842; and the Franciscan Handmaids of the Most Pure Heart of Mary founded by Mother Mary Theodore Williams in Savannah, Georgia (later relocating to Harlem, New York) in 1916. But in the 1940s and 1950s, historically white religious communities of women began to accept black candidates. Some of these religious communities had missions in urban and rural black communities and thus attracted vocations. However, most, if not all white religious communities were ill prepared to receive African American aspirants. While their intentions may have been good, they typically had no understanding of the history, culture, or religious experiences of the black community. Due to this lack of understanding, they most often lacked cultural sensitivity, and racial prejudices went unchecked. Bertha, Mississippi born and bred, entered the 1950s world of white, mostly native Wisconsin religious women who did not know how to meet her cultural and spiritual needs; nevertheless, they welcomed her. Bertha being black was not the only factor that differentiated her from her fellow aspirants. She had been reared in an upper-middle class household. Her parents were both college-educated and her father even further. Bertha was well educated and her skills had often exceeded her grade level. Her relatives were highly respected professionals within their communities. Most of the white aspirants' parents did not have college degrees, did not come from upper-middle class households, and often worked on dairy farms or in factories. Despite her background and pedigree, Bertha desperately wanted to fit in, be accepted, and prove that she was worthy to become a Franciscan Sister of Perpetual Adoration.

As with most black religious entering a majority white religious community, Bertha had to assimilate into the dominant white culture as a coping mechanism for survival and perseverance. Bertha would have been the first black person that most of her fellow aspirants ever met. Being the first and only black person to enter the La Crosse convent at the time, Bertha entertained insulting questions about her hair texture, skin color, and the entire black race. However, rather than complain, revolt, or leave the convent, she accepted it in order to be accepted. While Bertha had many fond memories of how loving, gracious, and accepting the white Franciscan sisters and Trinitarian priests at home in Canton had been to her, unfortunately it would be in the environment of a convent of white religious women that she would encounter the ugly face of racism and intolerance. Many black religious have attested that it was in the convent or seminary that they experienced racist behavior and prejudice for the very first time. Bertha was no exception.

Bertha's indomitable spirit, joy, and tenacity prevented her from succumbing to the occasional insensitivity and intolerance. Bertha wanted to become a professed Franciscan sister and she would face anything to meet her goal. She continued to make friends easily and loved establishing bonds of sisterhood with her classmates. In 1955, Bertha completed her course of study at St. Rose High School and entered Viterbo College, also in La Crosse. Being the daughter of college graduates, Bertha relished entering college. She wrote to her parents exclaiming, "College isn't so bad, but we do have tremendous assignments. I love speech. Did you ever think that I'd have to learn to talk? Well, I'm a college woman now!"[6]

The end of her aspirancy brought her to the beginning of her postulancy: a step closer to becoming an FSPA. The postulancy was the first formal step to becoming a professed Franciscan sister. The six-month postulancy was a time for Bertha and her classmates to learn the Rule and Constitutions of the Franciscan Sisters of Perpetual Adoration.[7]

As part of the instructions Bertha received on the history of the religious community she sought to enter, she learned that a group of twelve men and women of the Third Order Franciscans came from Bavaria to Milwaukee, Wisconsin, in May of 1849. Mother Aemiliana Dirr, the leader of the group of six women, was committed to founding a religious community of women dedicated to spreading the Gospel among German immigrants, educating their children, caring for their disadvantaged, and fostering adoration of the Blessed Sacrament. Having been diverted from their initial ministry to doing domestic work for the newly formed diocesan seminary, the discouraged foundress left the community. At the invitation of the first bishop of the newly formed Diocese of La Crosse, the new superior, Mother Antonia Herb, moved the sisters from Milwaukee to La Crosse in 1871. The sisters named their new motherhouse St. Rose of Viterbo Convent. In 1878, they were finally able to establish perpetual adoration of the Blessed Sacrament in their chapel in La Crosse and it has continued uninterrupted.[8]

The ministry of the Franciscan Sisters of Perpetual Adoration is expressed in their mission statement: "We are a community of vowed Franciscan women centered in Eucharist, committed to be loving presence through prayer, witness and service."[9] This loving presence that Bertha was drawn to as a child in Canton has manifested itself in many FSPA ministries, including care for orphans, education through parochial and diocesan schools, higher education, health care, domestic and foreign missions, and a variety of specialized ministries.

As a postulant attending classes at Viterbo College, Bertha was impressed by the school's strong fine arts curriculum.[10] She especially enjoyed the music and dramatic performances. Most likely singing and acting gave Bertha solace as she thought back to her childhood memories of singing and putting on plays for her neighborhood friends.

Bertha's excitement was short-lived when a serious health challenge brought her college studies to a halt. In the spring of 1955, during a routine physical, she tested positive for tuberculosis.[11] She was immediately confined to St. Francis Hospital across the street from the motherhouse. Sister Charlotte Bonneville, who had charge over the postulants, wrote to Dr. and Mrs. Bowman about their daughter's condition: "Since she is just across the street at St. Francis, I go to see her every day. She is amused at having to be in bed when she feels so well. She is very cheerful, too. We are praying that the x-ray is showing an old lesion and not a 'new' spot. . . . Bertha also wishes you to keep this a secret, although you may tell the sisters [La Crosse Franciscans in Canton] if you wish."[12]

Ongoing tests indicated that Bertha in fact had tuberculosis. The prescribed treatment of medications and chemotherapy caused nausea and vomiting for Bertha. To recover completely, she needed plenty of rest and relaxation. Her doctor insisted that she be sent to a sanatorium. The Bowmans consented to the doctor's recommendation and the Franciscan superiors admitted the very sick postulant to River Pines Sanatorium in Stevens Point, Wisconsin.

Charlene Smith and John Feister recount this frightening moment in young Bertha's life:

> For any seventeen-year-old to have tuberculosis was scary, let alone a black teenager in the segregated United States in 1955, a thousand miles from her Deep South home. Bertha, daughter of a doctor, understood her health had been compromised. She was determined to take whatever steps necessary to recover. She wrote a letter home and invited her mother to come visit. Mrs. Bowman traveled by train from Canton as she had for Christmas six months earlier. She accompanied Bertha in the ambulance from La Crosse to River Pines Sanatorium for Tuberculosis in Stevens Point, administered by the Sisters of St. Joseph. She was the first African American patient and first postulant from a religious community admitted in the history of River Pines Sanatorium.[13]

Throughout Bertha's convalescence at River Pines Sanatorium, she was an excellent patient. She faithfully followed the directives of her doctor and nurses. Everyone there enjoyed her joyful spirit and optimism during her sickness. To occupy her time, she continued to write letters and enrolled in a correspondence course in writing to keep up with her studies. As usual she continued to make new friends and to encourage the other patients in their recovery. She was finally released from the sanatorium in March of 1956, having spent almost a year in recovery. Bertha was eager to resume her studies and her postulancy, but due to her time away from the convent she was now a year behind her class and could not move ahead with them. Instead she would look forward to entering the novitiate with the class of 1958.[14]

The Franciscan Sisters of Perpetual Adoration required a period of two years for the canonical novitiate. This sacred time was for the novice to spend time growing in their understanding of religious life, the religious vows they would take, the community's history and charism, and Franciscan spirituality. At the end of these two years, the novice would profess her simple or temporary vows, which were renewed annually for three years, then once for three years, and finally they would make perpetual (lifetime) vows.[15]

Upon entering the novitiate, the novices would now be called sisters. Prior to the Second Vatican Council, sisters were assigned new names emphasizing their new state in life as set apart for God. Ordinarily, the sisters were given saints' names that had a special meaning to the community; it often was combined with Mary in honor of the Blessed Mother. On August 12, 1956, Bertha E. Bowman would no longer be the name by which this Canton native would be known. To her elation she was given the name Sister Mary Thea. Thea, the name of a little known fourth-century saint, meant "of God." It was also, of course, the feminine version of her beloved father's name, Theon.[16]

Novitiate could be a difficult time for a budding religious. In many ways, it was an initiation to see if a woman was authentically called to live the consecrated life. There were exacting rules and regulations that the new novices were expected to observe perfectly. The novice was given the complete religious habit, except for the black veil; the novice wore the habit with a white veil to symbolize purity.

Two years later, on August 12, 1958, in the Maria Angelorum Chapel, a twenty-year-old Sister Thea and nineteen other novices exchanged their white veils for the black veil of a professed sister of the Franciscan Sisters of Perpetual Adoration.[17] This was no ordinary profession ceremony; a black woman was becoming a professed sister for the first—and, in fact, only—time in this religious community's history. The *La Crosse Tribune* ran a photo of Sister Mary Thea in her full black habit, with the accompanying caption "First Negro." The accompanying article reported, "On August 12, the Franciscan Sisters of Perpetual Adoration of La Crosse will have their first professed colored member in the Community . . . Following her religious profession, Sister Thea will continue her studies at Viterbo College as a preparation for the teaching profession."[18] Dr. and Mrs. Bowman made the long journey to La Crosse and proudly beamed as they sat in the congregation during the profession Mass and witnessed their only child's dream come true. Dr. Bowman would not have the opportunity to make a wedding reception toast with the bottle of French champagne that he had purchased on the day his daughter was born. He could only embrace her and wish her well because she truly seemed happy becoming Sister Mary Thea Bowman, FSPA.

Thea worked vigorously to catch up and complete her college studies. Noting Thea's brilliance early on, her superior was certain that she would be a teacher. The post–World War II "baby boom" had produced a great demand for teachers.[19] Many religious communities of women had to place their newly professed sisters into classrooms even before they completed their bachelor of art degrees, and this was the case for Thea. In 1959 Thea received her first "mission slip" from reverend mother on the traditional FSPA "Appointment Day," which was observed annually on the feast of St. Anne, July 26. Thea's "mission slip" disclosed that she was being sent by "holy obedience" to teach fifth and sixth grade at Blessed Sacrament Catholic School in La Crosse. Blessed Sacrament was a school of white children. When the parents of the children learned that a colored sister would be teaching their children, they requested a meeting with the sister who served as principal to discuss this "urgent matter." In her wisdom, the principal did not meet with parents alone; she invited Thea to the meeting. And as it turned out, her infectious smile, warm personality, and Southern charm quickly alleviated all their fears.[20]

Years later, a newspaper reporter recounted Thea's comments about her early years teaching at Blessed Sacrament School:

> "I wasn't glad that I was there, but I felt deep in my heart that God had called me. I felt he had a reason for calling me, and that I had to wait on the Lord and be of good courage," she said.
>
> Her first teaching assignment was an affluent all-white parish in La Crosse, which she described as a happy experience. "The children liked me, and because the children liked me, the parents accepted me."
>
> Sister Thea remembers the time she met with a parent for a parent-teacher conference. The woman couldn't stop staring at her. "Finally, the woman says, 'You know, Christine talks about you all the time, but she never told us you were black.'"[21]

Immediately, Thea sought to establish a relationship between the white, Catholic students at Blessed Sacrament and the black, mostly non-Catholic students at her beloved Holy Child Jesus School in Canton. By sharing letters, stories, pictures, and experiences of life, the students began to build a bridge between two very different worlds. Thea believed that children could heal the racial divide in ways that perhaps their parents could not. From early on in her teaching career, Thea not only taught the required subject matter to her students, she also taught life lessons. She soon became a favorite teacher at Blessed Sacrament School.

The following year on Appointment Day, Thea's "mission slip" informed her that she would be returning to her fifth- and sixth-grade classroom at Blessed Sacrament School. She was delighted to go back to the place that she had forged good relationships with the staff and students alike. During the summers, Sister Thea would take summer courses to complete her undergraduate degree at Viterbo College.

At the end of her second year at Blessed Sacrament, Appointment Day rolled around once again. This time Thea's assignment was not a replication of the two previous years. Her mission slip announced an assignment that Thea had hoped and waited for: she was assigned to teach at Holy Child Jesus Mission School in Canton, Mississippi.[22] The overwhelming joy of this long-awaited assignment must have been quite evident on Thea's face. The required six weeks of attending classes at Viterbo College could not have ended fast enough for Sister Thea. It had been eight years since an impressionable teenager named Bertha left Canton, but now it was time for the matured young lady, Sister Mary Thea Bowman, to make the nine-hundred-mile journey back to the place that she knew and loved. Sister Thea was going home!

CHAPTER THREE

Returning to Canton (1961–1965)

How do we teach the poor that they can change their lives? How do we raise up the young men and women with the kind of confidence in themselves that says, "I am somebody; I am special?" Even if I am slow, even if I have a drug problem, even if my parents are gone, even if I don't have money, I'm somebody. And there are resources available in my community, and I have to reach out and grab those resources. And I say that of your child, how do we teach the children?[1]

Sister Thea Bowman, FSPA

South African Archbishop Desmond Tutu once described family this way: "You don't choose your family. They are God's gift to you as you are to them." These were probably the sentiments of Dr. and Mrs. Bowman as well as Thea as they anxiously awaited their reunion in Canton. It was 1961, and the twenty-three-year-old was excited and delighted to be back in the South and to embrace both the joy and challenge of educating children at her beloved alma mater, Holy Child Jesus Mission School. Thea knew that things would be different teaching in Canton than they were at Blessed Sacrament School in La Crosse. Besides the obvious racial difference, the white children in La Crosse had a newer learning classroom environment complete with new books, desks, equipment, and other learning resources. Thea, determined to fire-up her students with an eagerness to learn and to achieve, was ready for the challenge. Because she was a proud product of Holy Child Jesus Mission School, she wanted to give all that she had to nurture academic excellence, Christian virtues, and exemplary citizenship. She understood that a good educational foundation for these children could make the difference between an impoverished life or a life of success and accomplishment.

Though she was "home" in Canton, Thea would no longer live with her parents at their Hill Street residence, but with the sisters at the Franciscan convent on Garrett Street. Her domicile was not the only change that Thea had to face in coming home to the Jim Crow South. She arrived back in the midst of the turbulence of the civil rights movement. In La Crosse, she had been well aware of the movement, which included both violent resistance and the nonviolent protests of the Rev. Dr. Martin Luther King and other proponents of racial justice.

Thea sought ways that she could promote racial understanding and reconciliation in her own unique way. She often spoke of doing her "little bit" to make a difference in her community and with all whom she came in contact. This urgency to make a difference would be a steadfast commitment throughout her life. Years later Thea would reflect with a friend, the noted Mississippi author Margaret Walker:

> We were very conscious of the hostility of the [local] Southern white community and their objections to a black nun

living with white nuns in Canton. When I was riding with the white nuns, I would duck down in the car when we passed white people in the streets or on the roads—and especially when we passed the white police.

We talked a great deal about segregation and racism and worked hard for voter registration to combat these evils.[2]

During the mid-1960s, Canton became a hub of civil rights activity and the violent forces that opposed it. The town was the site of several notable marches, rallies, and meetings. During the "Freedom Summer" of 1964 a civil rights headquarters in Canton was bombed in an attack that fortunately killed no one, and the following year, black churches and homes in Canton were bombed. Dr. King was among many who came to Canton in June 1966 to participate in an event called the March against Fear. When activists tried to pitch a tent on the grounds of McNeal Elementary School, National Guard soldiers fired tear gas from the roof of the school into the crowd, injuring many.[3] Thea was not in Canton at the time, but Dr. King was among several activists who took refuge following the attack at Holy Child Jesus Church.

The sixties were not only a time of change and turbulence in the United States; the winds of change had also come to the Roman Catholic Church with the advent of the Second Vatican Council, which lasted for three years between 1962 and 1965. The Council ushered in many changes in the church, including within institutes of consecrated life of men and women. In 1962, the Franciscan Sisters of Perpetual Adoration changed the period for temporary vows from six years to five. This change affected Thea's vow class of 1958. To not take the sisters away from their mission assignments, formation classes would be held on designated weekends during the 1962–63 academic year at the motherhouse in

La Crosse. Sister Thea would have to make the long trip from Mississippi to join her fellow sisters for these mandatory sessions. In fact, because of the transition, Thea was in La Crosse the full summer of 1963 to continue with her degree-oriented summer school courses.

Thea had been asked her opinion about "the race problem" by many she encountered in La Crosse, and so in July 1963, she gave a presentation on "Negroes" and the purpose of the civil rights movement. This presentation made headline news in the Sunday edition of the local La Crosse newspaper. The article, titled "The Negro Needs Understanding," quotes Thea telling the newspaper reporter, "Naturally whites fear change, and they also are afraid the Negro will weaken American culture. These fears are not artificial, they are founded on facts. Negroes fear white dominance because they have experienced it. They fear rejection. They are barred from advancement. They cannot fulfill basic needs."[4] Her comments were insightful, assertive, and unapologetic. Soon she would be dedicating her life perpetually through vows to the Franciscan Sisters of Perpetual Adoration, but one could see that she was also deepening her lifelong commitment of being a voice for her people to bring understanding, peace, and justice.

Perpetual profession, the commitment by Sister Thea and her classmates to living as a Franciscan Sister of Perpetual Adoration for the rest of her life, took place at the motherhouse chapel in La Crosse on August 10, 1963.[5] Once again her parents made the trip to Wisconsin to lovingly support and encourage their only child. As a sign of her final vows, Thea received the signature medal that she would wear proudly even after she no longer wore the traditional habit.

With her formation completed, she went back to Canton with a renewed commitment to make sure that her students received a quality education. Thea's educational philosophy was poignant. She later described this philosophy in a 1988 television news interview, saying, "All I want to say is that everyone has a responsibility. We need to teach little children—the little five-year-old, the little four-year-old —that they can change things; they can make life better for themselves and for their family and for their country. And even though they can't vote at this time, they can be involved and participatory and contributing citizens."[6]

Upon her return to Holy Child Jesus Mission School, she was asked to move from teaching at the elementary school to the high school. Here she met a new challenge. Her students seemed disinterested in learning, especially the boys.

One of Thea's former high school students, Cornelia Johnson, first met Thea as her freshman year English teacher at Holy Child Jesus High School. Cornelia was fifteen years old and converted to Catholicism after having engaging conversations with Thea. Cornelia admitted that she wasn't interested in becoming a Catholic until she met Thea. She was amazed to meet a "black nun" who was so "down to earth" and loved the Lord. Cornelia recalled, "When Sister Thea taught English, she brought everything to life. She made me love literature. Sister Thea introduced me to Greek mythology and I was fascinated by it. I'm a bookworm today because of her. Reading opened a whole new world to me. She spoke to us not like children but as if we were her sisters and brothers. The students at Holy Child Jesus really knew that she cared about us."[7]

Cornelia remembered that the boys gave Sister Thea the most trouble initially but eventually she won them over. "The boys didn't want to read, so Sister Thea one day brought to class the 'funny pages' [the cartoon section of the newspaper] and told the boys to pick out their favorite comic character and to write why they found that character interesting. The boys enjoyed reading the funny pages so much, they eventually moved on to reading books. She was creative that way." Cornelia humorously recalled music class, saying, "she insisted that everyone could sing, and I tried to tell her that I couldn't sing. But she told me to open my mouth and sing, and I did! If Sister Thea told you that you could do something, you didn't argue with her, you just did it." Cornelia reminisced that she felt so comfortable talking to Sister Thea that sometimes she would stop by the convent after school to talk. "She was more than my teacher; she was my friend."[8]

Thea would later recall her days as a high school teacher to be her most taxing. She said, "I enjoyed it, but it was the hardest for me. You see, I was young when I started to teach high school. I was coming back to my hometown in Mississippi; there was a desperation in my teaching. There was an urgency in my teaching. I came home saying, 'You've got to learn!' "[9] "My daddy was convinced that if you could read, you could do anything. And I think he passed that conviction on to me."[10]

Thea had more success getting her high school students to love music and singing. Not only did the students at Holy Child Jesus High School enjoy singing with Thea, but they also were good singers. Thea harnessed their raw talent, trained their voices, developed their confidence and stage presence, and the Holy Child Jesus choir became bona fide performers. With continual practice and Thea's fine-tuning, in a few years her budding fifty-member choir was ready to record a record album. The album was a fundraising project to help the school raise desperately needed funds. It was called *The Voice of Negro America*. Sister Thea was the director, and Mr. C. W. Saulsbury was the accompanist who helped advise the recording.[11]

The album was a compilation of fourteen Negro spirituals highlighting the quest for freedom and the solace found in God and God's Word. Songs cherished within the spiritual tradition—including, "Go Down Moses," "Steal Away," and "Deep River"—were featured.[12] Students were thrilled to locate their names on the back of the album cover. These young Cantonite men and women felt a sense of accomplishment that they had never felt before. Thea had always told them that they were "somebody," and with the release of this album, they felt like they really were.

The album cover included a timely dedication: "To the promotion of brotherhood and universal peace." Besides singing on the album, Thea also offered commentary between each spiritual, explaining how that song offered hope and encouragement:

> Listen! Hear us! While the world is full of hate, strife, vengeance. We sing songs of love, laughter, worship, wisdom, justice, and peace because we are free. Though our forefathers bent to bear the heat of the sun, the strike of the lash, the chain of slavery, we are free. No man can enslave us. We are too strong, too unafraid. America needs our strength, our voices to drown out her sorrows, the clatter of war . . . Listen! Hear us! We are the voice of Negro America.[13]

The album was a great local success and sold many copies in the region, benefitting the school.

Getting yet a step closer to completing her bachelor's degree, Thea found herself during the summer of 1964 back at Viterbo College. While routine, she enjoyed the opportunity to study. She delved deeper into her love of language, writing, and English literature. Her skills as a talented communicator and writer were further developed through her own self-study and discipline, as well as from the guidance of Viterbo's stellar English faculty.

Upon returning to Canton and her teaching responsibilities at Holy Child Jesus High School in the fall, she continued to encourage her students to excel and to do their utmost best in all their subjects. She insisted that the phrase "I can't" should never be a part of a student's vocabulary. Yes, Thea was a demanding teacher. She was strict and stern when she felt that her students weren't willing to try to learn something new, but the students knew that her no-nonsense demeanor was an expression of love for them and for teaching. She once commented later in life:

> I love teaching. I like children. I think they are much more fun than adults. In a remarkable sort of way, children will believe you if you tell them your truth. Not that you have a corner on the truth, but if you tell them your truth, there's that intuitive grasp that children will believe you. If you love them, they will let you love them. I'm attracted to the freshness and beauty of young people. It is so important that they learn to value themselves before the world has had a chance to beat them down.[14]

Thea, being an only child, had very few relatives, but she had a cousin she was very close to and enjoyed the fact that they both were Catholics and vowed religious. Her cousin, Father Charles D. Burns, was a priest in the Society of the Divine Word, an international missionary religious community of priests and brothers. Fascinated by the valiant ministry being done by the Trinitarian priests and the Franciscan Sisters of Perpetual Adoration at Holy Child Jesus Mission, Father Burns wrote an article about it for the

Divine Word Messenger in 1965. Naturally Father Burns was also proud of the dedicated service that his beloved cousin Thea was also doing in her native Canton. The article focused particularly on the long-standing pastor (1960–79) of Holy Child Jesus Mission, Father Luke Mikschl, ST, and Thea. Titled "Deep in Their Hearts, Lord, They Do Believe," it offered valuable insights at what was the crux of ministry in the South during the tumultuous sixties. Burns wrote, "The Franciscan Sisters of Perpetual Adoration were willing and eager to claim the one in a thousand entry. Today Sister Thea is in the classrooms and on the playgrounds inspiring, enlightening and coaxing Negro youth to the basic realization that truly 'we shall overcome one day' but not without daily personal victories morally and intellectually. Sister Thea's realistic insight with regard to her students' social thinking and material inspirations adds another dimension to her teaching assets."[15]

In the article, Thea expounded on her concept of race relations and the need for racial justice:

> When I went back South, I still had a modicum of fear and mistrust—not for the white man in general but for the Southern white. Here in the South, I first got to know the clergy and religious who were from the South. I went to a neighboring region where there was one Sister who was from Mississippi. When I learned that she was from Mississippi, I thought, 'Let me out of here.' I was sure there was going to be trouble. However, this particular Sister was wonderful and made a special point of introducing me to all the priests and Brothers and Sisters in the area that were from the South. I learned volumes that weekend![16]

The article culminated with a quote from the nearly twenty-eight-year-old Thea expressing wisdom beyond her years and which would become her mantra throughout her life: "Cannot Americans, many and different, join hands in unity, live celestial harmony, establish a new and better world? For those who are members of the Church, the Mystical Body of Christ, this sharing of life is a spiritual obligation. The very word 'catholic' means 'all.' Jesus loved all men— and true love always tends to bring people together."[17]

Finally, after many years of diligent study, discipline and long trips north to Wisconsin, Thea completed the necessary requirements of Viterbo College in July 1965, earning her bachelor's degree in English.[18] With a great sense of accomplishment and an even greater zeal to learn more, this milestone would be the first of many in Thea's educational matriculations.

CHAPTER FOUR

From Canton to the Nation's Capitol (1966–1972)

My approach is: teach me. I will learn. I want to learn. I want to keep on learning until I die. But I also want to teach. I want to accept your gifts. Please share your treasures with me, but I also want to share my treasures with you.[1]

Sister Thea Bowman, FSPA

Completing her undergraduate degree was only the beginning of Thea's pursuit of knowledge and the trajectory of her educational endeavors. She incessantly wanted to seek, to ponder, to investigate the unknown. Learning was a delight for Thea; the more she learned, the more she wanted to know. Her quest for erudition was insatiable. For Thea, understanding and comprehension were her best friends and wisdom was her soul mate. In the balmy month of June 1966, Thea traveled to the nation's capitol to attend the prestigious Catholic University of America (CUA). Many religious communities of women attended CUA and the campus was surrounded with houses of formation and continuing education. The Franciscan Sisters of Perpetual Adoration were no exception. While they did not own their own house of study in Washington, the FSPAs had several sisters boarding with another religious community. Thea was eager to begin classes toward earning her master of arts degree in English.

She found her classes at CUA both challenging and enjoyable. More challenging was trying to balance time between her classes, keeping up with her reading assignments, writing papers, attending community prayers and meals, forming community with her fellow sisters, and making new friends. Thea managed to multitask all the requirements of her time and energy in a given day. Initially, she had to forego the many invitations to go out socially or to visit friends at their homes, as she was aware that doing well in her classes was the first priority of being at CUA.

Gradually Thea began to venture out into the city that was the apex of political power and governance. Among blacks, Washington was nicknamed "Chocolate City," because of its historically large black population. Living in a mostly black town was not new to Thea. What was novel for her was that these black Washingtonians were neither typically Southern nor rural. The black community in Washington was a conglomeration of upper-middle class, middle class, working poor, and very poor; well-educated and poorly educated; business owners and those employed in every occupation imaginable; those who were Muslim, Buddhist, Protestants of all denominations, and unbelievers. What piqued Thea's interest most and was a cause of her joy and excitement was that she found in Washington a large black Catholic community. Studying in the District of Columbia would be far different than her summers pursuing her bachelor's degree in Wisconsin.

Living in Washington exposed her not only to black people from across the continental United States but also to people of African descent from Africa, the Middle East, and the Caribbean. Thea had read about and studied pan-African culture, customs, and traditions, but this personal contact and the bonds of friendship she formed greatly enhanced all that she had learned. Thea not only felt that she now belonged to an extended family that made her feel comfortable and "at home," but that she had found people with whom she could identify, and thus her spirit and spirituality was enlivened and reinvigorated. She loved the various ethnic foods, music, dance, literature, stories, artistic expressions, and cultural attire of people of the African Diaspora. She was nearly a thousand miles away from her beloved Canton, but in Washington she felt very much at home.

Black Catholics had a long and significant history in the city. The sheer number of black Catholics was impressive; unlike the solitary Holy Child Jesus Catholic Church in Canton, Washington in the 1960s had several vibrant black Catholic churches and schools. With the advent of Vatican II, these black Catholic faith communities had begun incorporating the richness of their African American culture, music, and traditions into their liturgies. Spirituals, traditional black hymns, and traditional and contemporary gospel music had taken their places in Catholic choir lofts and choir stands and were making a joyful noise unto the Lord! Black Catholic laity, clergy, and religious sisters and brothers warmly welcomed Thea to the city.

Thea was given permission by her religious community to begin working on her master's degree and eventually her doctoral degree full time beginning the fall of 1968 at CUA. For convenience, she moved into Shields Hall for graduate students, located on Michigan Avenue, across from the main campus. While living there, Thea experienced something that would impact her life and her future ministry: an African friend committed suicide. This friend had tried to share her stress and pain with Sister Thea, but she at the time had failed to perceive the trouble in her friend.[2] Her friend's suicide lingered with her, because she deeply regretted not being "present" or realizing the confusion and pain her friend was in. The suicide was so devastating for her that she resolved to be present to those in need of her time and attention and to genuinely listen to words spoken and unspoken. Empathy became a deep-seated virtue of Thea's for the rest of her life. She made a personal vow to share her boundless love and joy with others and to be observant of those around her who were sad, neglected, or downtrodden.

Not only would Thea become increasingly empathetic, but also her DC environment opened for her a new lease on life. She had never been reclusive or withdrawn, but she felt a new need to be her authentic self. Her formation as a Franciscan Sister of Perpetual Adoration had instilled in her all the attributes of being a faithful religious woman, but now Thea resolved to be her *true* self while being a religious. Thea realized there was no dichotomy between being a vowed religious woman and a strong, conscious black woman. She didn't have to be one or the other, but rather she would be "both/and." She had moved away from the one-sided notion of assimilating and integrating and knew that she had gifts to share with her religious community, the church, and with all she met.[3] She would often say later in life, in her preaching and teaching, "You have gifts to share, and I don't mind receiving your gifts. But I have gifts, too, that I want to share with you." She particularly wanted to share the beautiful gifts of her African and African American culture. There was no singular pivotal moment that brought her this greater cultural consciousness, but between the shock of her friend's suicide and the blatant racial injustices in the 1960s, Thea was jolted to be her beautiful, black self and to teach and preach about the richness and giftedness of her black cultural heritage. The devastating suicide of her African friend and the many lives lost in the violence against black bodies on rural roads and urban streets brought a renewed or new life for Thea.

A year of defiant protests occurred around the country in 1968. People took to the streets of major cities to protest the war in Vietnam, racism, inequality, poverty, and nuclear weapons proliferation, and to support women's rights, civil liberties, and protection of the environment. In this context, black Catholic clergy and religious women joined their voices with others to call for justice both in the church and society. Black clergy and scholars made racism a central focus of their pastoral and theological work. A formal statement released by the National Black Catholic Clergy Caucus in 1968[4] and a notable book by priest and theologian Lawrence Lucas in 1970[5] both made the daring accusation that the Catholic Church is "a white racist institution."

Writing at a major meeting in Detroit just days after the assassination of Dr. King, the National Black Catholic Clergy Caucus further asserted, "Within the ghetto, the role of the Church is no longer that of spokesman and leader. Apart from a more direct spiritual role, the Church's part must now be that of supporter and learner. This is a role that white priests in the black community have not been accustomed to playing and are not psychologically prepared to play." And among their nine-point list of demands that they made to the Catholic Church, the Clergy Caucus called for "dioceses to provide centers of training for white priests intending to serve and survive in black communities."[6]

Attending the Detroit meeting was a defining moment for many black priests and brothers. It was emphatically a clarion call defining who they were as black Catholic priests and religious brothers and denouncing the evil of racism in the church.

There was one black religious sister present at the meeting in Detroit, Sister Martin de Porres (Patricia Muriel) Grey, a Sister of Mercy (RSM). Grey left the meeting determined to found an organization for black religious sisters to address their personal needs as well as to confront the racism of the church and in the nation.[7] Grey sent letters to all the black sisters in the country, inviting them to come to a meeting at Carlow College in Pittsburgh, which was operated by her religious community, the Sisters of Mercy. The black sisters also received the blessing and gracious hospitality of Bishop John J. Wright, the Bishop of Pittsburgh, to host the seminal meeting in his diocese. Over 150 black Catholic religious women came to Carlow from 79 national and international congregations, acknowledging "the pressing demand for black religious to address themselves to the urgent need for the Catholic Church in America to develop greater relevancy for black folk, or to risk losing its credibility as a manifestation of Christian unity. The Holy Spirit moved Sister Martin de Porres [now Patricia Grey, PhD] to call black religious women to share in a task, that would be done only by black religious women acting together, fully free and joyously for the coming of the kingdom."[8] The fruit of the meeting was the founding of the National Black Sisters' Conference in August 1968.

Thea received her invitation and attended the inaugural meeting of the National Black Sisters' Conference in Pittsburgh; she is, then, rightly called a founding member of this organization. She was ready to provide vision and leadership for this determined group of black religious women. Once again, the timing was right for Thea to share her gifts, her wisdom, and her infectious joy with the young organization.

A photo of Thea singing at the meeting went out across the country through the National Catholic News wire.[9] Undoubtedly, Thea had found the black sisterhood, support, and encouragement that she longed for and that sustained her throughout the rest of her life. The National Black Sisters' Conference was likewise blessed to count Sister Thea among their ranks.

The confidence and reassurance reaped from being a part of the foundation of the National Black Sisters' Conference only confirmed and deepened Thea's commitment to be a catalyst for the voiceless, neglected, and unheard. The gathering of like minds, shared visions, and collaborative support impelled her to tell her story—the story of her people's sorrow and joy, struggle and strength, and their quest and demand for justice. She would use what God had given her, her voice in spoken and sung word, her mind and its astute intelligence and capacity for creativity and cleverness, her spirit and spirituality that witnessed her walk with God, and her body that dramatically painted pictures and drew attention to her joy, inner peace, and abundant love. Thea, ever capable of doing more than one thing at the same time, would occasionally move from her studies to the stage to tell her people's story. Increasingly, invitations came for her to give lectures and presentations on the Negro spirituals and oral literature tradition. The Catholic University of America was one of the first places to recognize Thea as not only a graduate student but also competent teacher and invited her to teach black literature on campus. This opportunity led to a deluge of speaking engagements. Most notably, she was invited to speak at the historically black and private university, Howard University, in 1968, soon after Dr. Martin Luther King Jr. was assassinated.[10] Titled "The Negro in Education," it was an early address that helped launch what would become an ongoing ministry of sharing her story:

> By our achievement, our accomplishment, our success we prove to America that black power is responsible, productive, progressive. Black power is one of her most treasured assets that she can no longer afford—in the words of Frederick Douglass—to let her strong black arm hang helpless at her side. I know that the younger generation is ready to do something for civil rights. Our young people have risked their lives to attend meetings, to march, to boycott, to demonstrate, to sit in. These things are useful and good. But I'm asking our young people for something better and something bigger. How many of you the educated, the elite, are willing to prepare yourselves to lead? To write for your people? To speak for your people? To represent us in the courtroom? To see that justice is done?
>
> Martin Luther King is dead. Will you speak for us, write for us, organize, lead? Will you lead us into the Promised Land?"[11]

Keeping focused on her primary purpose for being in Washington, Thea completed and submitted her master's thesis to the Graduate School of Arts and Sciences at CUA in January of 1969. It was titled, "A Complete Explication and Critical Analysis of the 'Ruful Lamentacio of the Deth of Quene Elisabeth' by Sir Thomas More."[12] In May of 1969, she was awarded a master of arts degree in English from the university.

While pleased with the thought and long hours devoted to completing her master's degree, she turned her attention to earning her doctorate. She immersed herself in disciplined research, study, and writing during the academic years of 1969 through 1972. Thea had a fascination with the life, fortitude, integrity, and writings of Sir (Saint) Thomas More and chose one of his treatises as the focal point of her doctoral dissertation. More "spoke" to the core of who she was; she resonated with his spirit, wit, humor, commitment to family and truth, and endurance. Thea was both passionate and intrigued by Sir Thomas More's life and his literary acumen. She chose to concentrate her dissertation on one of More's final works, *A Dyalogue of Comforte Agaynste Tribulacyon*.[13]

Biographers Smith and Feister wrote, "*A Dyalogue of Comforte Agaynste Tribulacyon* appealed to Thea's wise empathic spirit. She saw in it More's attempt to comfort his family, his friends, and himself while at the same time explaining how suffering is necessary sometimes to get what we want. Fortunately for Thea, *A Dyalogue of Comforte Agaynste Tribulacyon* had not previously been the subject of much scholarly analysis."[14]

Sister Thea titled her dissertation "The Relationship of Pathos and Style in *A Dyalogue of Comforte Agaynste Tribulacyon*: A Rhetorical Study." She successfully defended it in April 1972. According to Smith and Feister, "In what her professors found to be a generally brilliant work, Sister Thea explores how Thomas More used pathos—'essaying to move the will by confronting each passion with its proper object' to comfort his family and friends while imprisoned and awaiting execution in the Tower of London. It is a deep, technical and enlightening study, inspired, in part, by her early preoccupation with More."[15]

Dr. Theon and Mary Bowman, as well as those who knew and loved her back home, rejoiced that there was another Dr. Bowman from Canton, Mississippi—Dr. Thea Bowman!

CHAPTER FIVE

Viterbo College: Professor Bowman (1972–1978)

One of the things I learned about students in college
is that so many come there programmed to find out
what the teacher wants and what the teacher wants
them to think and what the teacher wants them to
say. I say you don't have to do that. You don't have
to be afraid. Think for yourself. Your opinion is as
good as mine. So long as you support your opinion
by evidence, it is as valid as mine. That's my approach. You've got it, then use it.[1]

Sister Thea Bowman, FSPA

To express their elation and pride over their daughter's
achievement, Thea's parents gave her and several of her
sisters a trip to Europe. It would serve as a prologue to a
three-week seminar in English literature that Thea would
attend at Oxford University. The journey would take Thea
and her companions to cities in Germany, Austria, France,
Italy, Greece, and the United Kingdom. She was beguiled by
the antiquity of the continent's places and artifacts and

captivated by the languages and customs of the various ethnicities she encountered. While Thea found each city unique and fascinating, she gleaned deeper insights of her religious community, the Franciscan Sisters of Perpetual Adoration, as she explored the culture and traditions of Germany. Biographers Smith and Feister observe, "Until she actually went to Germany, Thea's impression of the German work ethic and Germans was that they were serious, efficient, dour, somewhat off-putting, frugal, emotionally unexpressive. The clash of her own southern upbringing upon entering a primarily German community had been, in some respects, piercing. Meeting actual Germans in their homeland afforded her an entirely different perspective. With their friendliness, warmth, gaiety, exuberant personalities, the German locals enthralled her."[2]

Yet another place that had a significant impact on Thea was her visit to the German concentration camps. Smith and Feister note that Thea could not get Dachau out of her thoughts: "I still think of the pictures, the sights we saw at Dachau—rooms built for sixty into which four hundred Jews were crowded, whipping block, public square for roll call and punishment, pictures of prisoners hanged by their wrists or forced to stand for hours in the sun or during slave labor, or going to a gas chamber, or so starved they looked like skeletons, used as human guinea pigs, thrown into open mass graves, piles of dead naked bodies, fillings ripped from teeth. I think I'll never forget it."[3]

The traveling Franciscan sisters arrived in Assisi, Italy, on July 2, 1972.[4] Assisi was the home of St. Francis and the spiritual home of every Franciscan. Thea was drawn to all the holy sites related to St. Francis and St. Clare in Assisi, including their final resting places. Surely, being in this significant town of Franciscan history and spirituality must have renewed her commitment to the Franciscan way of life. From Assisi, the sisters drove to Rome, where they visited the Vatican (and enjoyed a public audience with Pope Paul VI), the Pantheon, the city's major churches, the Coliseum, and other famous sites.[5]

Being a scholar of English literature, Thea was awestruck upon her arrival in the United Kingdom. Ever adaptable, she changed her focus to the studies ahead of her. Thea audited a course on "The Individual in the Novel" with six other students. She was bolstered with meeting students from several countries. Typically, she studied and engaged her fellow classmates as much as she learned from the subject matter. She confidently met and exceeded all that was required of being in this once-in-a-lifetime course.

With great zeal Professor Bowman began her new role teaching English at Viterbo College in La Crosse in the fall of 1972. She gripped her students' attention and captivated them by her knowledge and ability to assist them in becoming better writers, thinkers, and communicators. At Viterbo, Thea taught courses in English, black literature, and history. She was a noted authority on Sir Thomas More and William Shakespeare, as well as southern writers like Eudora Welty and William Faulkner.[6] She continued to offer lectures on Negro music and culture around the surrounding areas. She organized a group of singers called the Hallelujah Singers, which, although predominantly white, performed Negro spirituals with Thea as their leader and guide.[7] She believed that her culture and enriching music was a gift not to be hidden but to be shared with others. The Hallelujah Singers were well received on the Viterbo campus and throughout the community.

Thea eventually became the head of Viterbo's English department. While she was well respected as a teacher and scholar among the faculty and students alike, her teaching skills and ability to build bridges across cultures could not be contained to the campus. During her six-year tenure at Viterbo, she accepted many invitations to talk to various groups near and far, especially on the topic of race.

The July 9, 1973, edition of the *La Crosse Tribune* included an article that was headlined, "Soul Food, Dance Help Introduce Black Writings." It reported:

> Sister Thea Bowman, head of the English department at Viterbo and a black, organized the project. Sister Thea said she considered it vital for Americans to know the literature of blacks and Chicanos, Indians and Orientals. She urged inclusion of black literature as part of high school and college offerings in literature, not as a separate course. She reported black literature and authors are virtually unknown to most white Americans, who rarely had such information included even as part of college-level studies.[8]

The Daily Sentinel (Woodstock, Illinois), on March 7, 1974, anticipated a concert Thea was to perform. The article reported, "'The Negro spiritual and the Black Man's Response to God' discusses the spiritual as rhetoric with particular emphasis on the spiritual as an expression of the black man's consciousness. Sister Thea hopes by her singing to preserve the old songs whereby Black Americans through the centuries have praised God, offered comfort to brothers and eased the pain of life's trying situations. She also hopes by her musical outpouring to spread the Gospel message of faith, peace and love."[9]

The July 19, 1974, edition of the *La Crosse Tribune* reported on Thea and the Hallelujah Singers' efforts to raise desperately needed funds to keep Holy Child Jesus School open in Canton, Mississippi:

> In [1947] the Franciscan Sisters of Perpetual Adoration opened a school for the educationally deprived people of Canton.

Now, Sister Thea said, "Holy Child Jesus School is experiencing the same kind of financial difficulties that have forced the closing of many private schools in the South at a time when they are most needed." . . .

"One of the greatest contributions that educators can make to the black man's struggle for equality is to share the results of their education," Sister Thea said.[10]

Thea believed it was one thing to talk about racial strife and race relations, but it was important to move beyond conversation to direct interaction and commitment to bring about true and lasting change. She was convinced that at the root of racism was ignorance due to lack of personal engagement and interpersonal communication. Thea was fond of teaching beyond book knowledge and often sought to teach experientially. Experiences, she conjectured, enabled students to learn new ideas and to gain new impressions subjectively, so she sought to get her students out of the classroom and into the "real world" to have first-hand encounters. One such encounter was a study trip to Mississippi, with the dual purpose of studying southern writers and getting better acquainted with black people there. Thea arranged for her students to live in the homes of black people and to experience their food and customs. The May 4, 1975, *La Crosse Tribune* reported Thea's innovative learning experiences under the headline "Trip Is Experience in Hostility":

Through the shock of discrimination, segregation and potential physical violence, the Viterbo College students who toured the South during Easter vacation kept one thing in mind—it was an experience. . . .

[Sister Thea said,] "When we went down there, there was still separate rooms for whites and Negroes. When we walked on the sidewalk, Negroes stepped off so we could pass. Because the students lived with black families while in Mississippi, they experienced what the black experienced. That experience was mainly hostility."[11]

From 1976 through 1978, Thea balanced her increasingly busy speaking schedule with her classes and English department responsibilities. Requests poured in for her to give lectures, concerts, retreats and workshops, and her scope had grown from regional to national. Her topics ranged from Negro spirituals, to black religion and the arts, to religious education and teaching methodologies. Finding that she was energized by her speaking commitments, she rarely rejected a request to speak. She kept her audiences mesmerized by her uncanny ability to have her listeners at the same time intrigued by her knowledge, delighted at her folksy southern humor, and tearful as her singing and preaching reached deep into their memories and feelings.

Thea loved teaching at Viterbo College and being amid the impressionable young college students. But the more aware she became of her cultural identity, her rootedness in her black cultural heritage, and her need for the space to freely express herself, she knew that her time of living and teaching in La Crosse was coming to an end. Once at a day of recollection with other FSPA professors she lived with on the fifth floor of Viterbo's Murphy Center, Thea completed a reflection questionnaire, and her responses indicated feelings of loneliness and feeling misunderstood by some of the sisters in her community. Here are the reflection questions and her answers:

> I feel most comfortable at home when I am:
> *At home in Mississippi or with people who understand me; with black folks and Indians and Orientals and Latinos or with kids any age or color.*

At work, I am:
Energetic, self-confident, happy (except for meetings and desk work), efficient, domineering sometimes, more crazy and open about feelings, theatrical.

At home (Murphy Center fifth floor):
Often afraid I'll make a noise and disturb my neighbor, restrained, crabbed, restricted, confined, angry

When out with my friends, I am:
Silly if I feel like it; at ease, listening, talkative[12]

At the end of the academic semester of 1978, Thea received her new assignment to return home to Canton.[13] Dr. and Mrs. Bowman were older, growing frail, and needed assistance. Her religious community understood that it was necessary for her to go back and care for her elderly parents. Before heading south, Thea had a lot of business to attend to, including community meetings, her annual retreat, speaking engagements, applying for a job in the Diocese of Jackson, Mississippi, packing, saying good-byes, farewell parties, and one last summer Shakespeare course to teach.[14] Professor Bowman had made a tremendous impact on many lives while in the classroom at Viterbo College. She knew that her teaching days were far from over. But now it was time for the devoted daughter to go back home and care for her aging parents who had made many sacrifices on her behalf. Although she was going back to Canton with some uncertainty about her future, she resolutely journeyed home assured that God would make everything alright.

CHAPTER SIX

Returning to Her Roots, Race, and Old Time Religion
(1978–1984)

> African people became African Americans. Relating
> and communicating, teaching and learning, loving,
> and expressing faith in the God who loves and
> saves, they embodied and celebrated themselves and
> their values, goals, dreams, and relationships.[1]
>
> Sister Thea Bowman, FSPA

It has been said that one's home is where one's mother
and father live. In Thea's case, then, home was still at 136
Hill Street in Canton, Mississippi, a place she first left when
she was fifteen years old, but which now beckoned her back.
Her mother, now nearly seventy-six years old, had been sick
for some time. Her father was nearly eighty-four. It was
clear that at his advanced age, he could no longer care for
his wife by himself. When Dr. Bowman himself became ill,
it was time for Thea to return to Canton. Thea's devotion
to her parents meant that anything else she was doing was

secondary to their care. She moved into her childhood home to live with her parents once again. But even as Thea remained faithful to caring for her aging and infirmed parents, the demands for her preaching, teaching, sage wisdom, and leadership to an emerging black Catholic movement and consciousness were increasing.

Returning to Mississippi in 1978, she found that there were some advances in terms of race relations and yet there remained racial strife, segregation, intolerance, and a desperate need for racial reconciliation in the Magnolia State. She knew that she could not remain still or silent in the face of inequality and injustice.

The Roman Catholic Diocese of Jackson was being led at the time by Bishop Joseph Brunini, a native Mississippian whose father was Italian and mother was Jewish. He knew racial injustice first-hand and in those years just after the Second Vatican Council, he was not timid about pushing for change within both the church and society. Indeed, the *New York Times* had called him a "risk-taking bishop."[2] Bishop Brunini courageously integrated the Catholic schools in Mississippi, to the fierce consternation of many white Catholics. He was a strong voice in addressing issues of ecumenism, evangelization, racism, poverty, and social justice. He assisted in establishing the interfaith Mississippi Religious Leadership Conference in 1970 and served as its first chairman.[3] He was a fair and just man concerned about the needs of racial minorities, most especially black Catholics. Bishop William Houck succeeded Brunini as bishop of the Diocese of Jackson in 1984 and continued much of the work on racial justice he had begun. Both Brunini and Houck were friends and admirers of Thea. Likewise, she admired and respected their vision and leadership of the church in Mississippi. Recalling the hiring of Sister Thea to be director of the diocesan Office for Intercultural Awareness, Bishop Houck recalled in an interview, "I think it was Bishop Brunini's idea, that here was a wonderful black woman who was talented, who had her doctorate in English, a native daughter of Holy Child Jesus Parish. . . . Since she was going to be living here, encourage her to join the diocese staff and give her that responsibility of arranging awareness about all people and the cultural diversity in the Church."[4]

First as consultant to and then as director of the Office for Intercultural Awareness, Thea saw new opportunities to use her talents to break down the nefarious walls of racial prejudice. Brunini entrusted this monumental task to Thea because he knew that her persuasive and disarming personality, her astute intellect, and her evident holiness would help her bring about genuine unity in the midst of diversity. Thea's ability to communicate was key. She was known for assessing a situation before she moved forward. When she spoke at conferences in ballrooms or auditoriums, in church halls or church basements, in boardrooms or in classrooms, she posed simple questions with important answers in her disarming southern, folksy manner, told stories with significant moral lessons, and sang, always sang, in ways that defused tension and made spectators into participants. Never monolithic or predictable in her approach to bringing cultural awareness, Thea always told what she called the "true truth." She told her audiences what needed to be said. Her confidence in herself and in her messages came from a place of prudent discernment, fervent prayer, and above all, plain old common sense. Years later, she told an interviewer,

> I learned survival. I'm from Mississippi, and people who did not learn to contain their anger and frustration did not live long. You learn very early on how to wear the mask

so that if I had to work with you and I felt—not that I knew—that you were racist in your heart, I learned to guard my manner, to guard my speech, even to guard my thoughts, my feelings, passions, and emotions. I did that not because I hated you, but because I had to survive. I did that because my people had to have a job, because their children had to walk in safety.[5]

Thea continued:

I walk in a number of different communities, just like my Native American brothers and sisters and my Hispanic brothers and sisters, my Asian brothers and sisters; we have to walk in more than one world. When I come into the world of academe, or when I come into the world of business, or when I come into the world of politics or statesmanship, or into the world of international conversation, I have to be bilingual, bicultural. I have to be able to talk your talk and talk it better than you can, if I am going to be accepted and respected by many people in your society.[6]

Thea made regular reports to the bishop on her work in the Diocese of Jackson. She was committed to implementing the mandate of Bishop Brunini, namely to "(1) try to help improve inter-racial relations in the diocese; (2) to try to help black schools in their self-help programs; and (3) possibly to undertake some activities designed to foster black vocations."[7] Understanding music as a nonintrusive way of introducing culture and interacting with culture, she shared some ideas in writing with the bishop: "In September I would like to try to establish a Diocesan Gospel Choir, (1) to sing at liturgies; (2) to promote appreciation of black life and culture; (3) to provide entertainment; (4) to serve as a bonding organization for blacks in the diocese."[8] Bishop Brunini was supportive of her national speaking ministry. Through her lectures, workshops, concerts, and revivals, Thea drew attention to the intercultural awareness and evangelization efforts, especially in the black community, in the Diocese of Jackson. Her highly effective and progressive ministry served as a model to be replicated in archdioceses and dioceses throughout the country.

Prior to Thea coming on the scene to promote indigenous worship, singing, and preaching from an African American Catholic perspective, there was a black priest of the Archdiocese of Cincinnati who was the herald of black Catholic liturgical music and worship. His name was Father Clarence Joseph Rufus Rivers Jr. (1931–2004). In 1956, Father Rivers had become the first black priest ordained for the Archdiocese of Cincinnati. He earned his doctoral degree in liturgy and made a significant impact in the liturgical reform in the United States after the Second Vatican Council. He was devoted to African American culture and was known for his distinctive, African-inspired liturgical vestments. Father Rivers was most noted for the liturgical music he composed, beginning with his "An American Mass Program," which combined Gregorian chant with the melodic patterns and rhythms of traditional Negro spirituals. His most popular hymn was "God is Love." He first sang the song at the National Liturgical Conference in 1964, and received a ten-minute standing ovation when he had finished.[9] Thea and Father Clarence were kindred spirits, and so it was not surprising that he would ask her to write one of the introductions of his seminal book on black Catholic worship, *The Spirit in Worship* (1978).

In 1978, as Thea was immersed in promoting cultural awareness and articulating the richness of black culture, theology, language and literature, worship styles, and music, yet another major black Catholic organization was conceived.

On October 12 through 15, black Catholic clergy and vowed religious women and men from varied academic and pastoral disciplines gathered in Baltimore, Maryland, at the motherhouse of the Oblate Sisters of Providence to articulate through papers and dialogue a unique black Catholic theology.[10] Most if not all were members of the National Black Catholic Clergy Caucus and National Black Sisters' Conference, but those organizations were primarily concerned with pastoral matters. Many of the black priests, brothers, and sisters forming this new organization had obtained or were pursuing terminal degrees in theology or related disciplines and belonged to Catholic theological societies that welcomed them but were not discussing theology germane to the black Catholic experience. Capuchin Father Thaddeus J. Posey had called this new group together, which adopted the name Black Catholic Theological Symposium (BCTS). Sister Thea was among the thirty-three participants who gathered for that inaugural meeting at the Oblate Sisters' headquarters. While she did not present a paper at this initial meeting, she was elated to participate with her academic colleagues, many of whom were close friends.

The result of this nascent meeting was not only the creation of a new entity but also a new theological journal. The first proceedings of the BCTS were edited by Father Posey and published as *Theology: A Portrait in Black*. Because of its rich green cover, it came to be affectionately called "the green book." Blessed Sacrament Father Joseph R. Nearon, systematic theologian and professor at John Carroll University, in his introduction explained the purpose of the BCTS and the import of a black Catholic theology:

I see this Black Catholic Theological Symposium as a real contribution to American Catholic Christianity in these waning years of the twentieth century. I also see our gathering—as a real contribution to Black Theology. Until now, as we all know Black Theology has almost entirely been restricted to the Protestant tradition. I am convinced that we, not so much because we are Black, but because we belong to the Catholic tradition have an approach that can enrich this whole enterprise called Black Theology. We have an obligation both because we are Black and because we are Catholic to share this with our brothers and sisters, Black, White, Catholic and Protestant.

In a word, prompted by the Holy Spirit we say to our people and to our Church: you need us and because we love, we are not going to fail you.[11]

In the midst of her involvement in these new organizations and the development of her local and national ministries, Thea remained attentive to the health and well being of her parents. As it became increasingly difficult for her to be at her office in Jackson and also keep speaking engagements locally and nationally, she sought dependable assistance to help her care for her parents. Sister Dorothy Ann Kundinger, FSPA, was assigned in 1979 to teach at Holy Child Jesus School in Canton. A native of Wisconsin and affectionately known as "Dort," Kundinger was a few years behind Thea in religious profession. She hadn't gotten to know Thea well during their formation years in La Crosse, because sisters associated mostly with their fellow classmates. She became better acquainted with Thea because when she was traveling locally for speaking engagements, she would call the convent and ask if someone wanted to drive along with her. Sister Dort recalled, "Of course I would jump at the opportunity to go with Thea because I was new to Mississippi and thought what a wonderful way to see the State and get to know people."[12] The many road trips for her presentations provided time for meaningful conversations and getting better acquainted. It also served as the beginning of a cherished friendship. When Thea had to travel outside of Mississippi, Sister Dort drove her to the airport and at times checked in on Dr. and Mrs. Bowman while their daughter was away. Most days after teaching class Dort went to the Bowman home to see if they needed anything. Dort's presence with her parents was a great relief for Thea.

Thea rejoiced at receiving the news that her good friend and fellow Franciscan, Father James Patterson Lyke, was appointed as an auxiliary bishop of the Diocese of Cleveland. She was invited to sing a communion meditation song at the ordination liturgy on August 1, 1979. In her inveterate manner, she stirred the hearts of those gathered with her melodious soprano voice. It was after that Mass when Sister Eva Marie Lumas, SSS, first met Thea:

> People were walking out of the cathedral and I was standing in the back and a woman comes up to me and says, "Oh Sister Thea, your song was so beautiful!" Now Thea was at least seven inches taller than I am and a browner hue than I am. Now I didn't know that Thea was standing a few feet behind me and overheard the woman . . . and before I could say you have me mistaken, Thea answered the woman and said, "Wasn't it?" I turned around and there she is and we both get a chuckle out of it. And the woman walks away. And that's how we met and we had a chance to talk more later at the reception.[13]

This was the beginning of a very close relationship that spanned the spectrum of teacher and student, mentor and mentee, and collaborators, but above all, cherished confidants and beloved friends.

In November of 1979, the US Catholic bishops approved a long-awaited national pastoral letter on racism, entitled *Brothers and Sisters to Us*. Bishop Joseph A. Francis, SVD, auxiliary bishop of the Archdiocese of Newark, was influential in bringing this important document to the full body of bishops. Black Catholics in America had wondered for years if their bishops understood the enduring negative effects that racism had on people of color. The opening sentences of the pastoral letter seek to offer some assurance that the bishops are cognizant of its evils: "Racism is an evil which endures in our society and in our Church. Despite apparent advances and even significant changes in the last two decades, the reality of racism remains. In large part it is only the external appearances which have changed."[14] Thea undoubtedly welcomed this supportive pastoral letter from the bishops, and little did she know at the time that she would one day remind them of what they said in 1979.

During the early 1980s, Thea was annually invited to speak at the William Faulkner Conference hosted by the University of Mississippi in Oxford, Mississippi, Faulkner's home. The conference was cosponsored by the university's Center for the Study of Culture and its English Department. Thea relished the opportunity while in pastoral ministry to turn her attention for a time back to academia and southern American literature. She was fascinated by Faulkner's approach to themes like racism, violence, and white supremacy. One year she delivered a musical presentation on "Black Music and Culture in the Works of William Faulkner." She noted, "I see this conference as a place where you come in contact with the world he created. In Faulkner's world, black people are always present. Some of his most compassionate and strong characters are black. Even his use of the black church is symbolic of transcendence and strength. He uses blacks as a combination of reality and symbolism."[15]

Also during the 1980s, the Institute for Black Catholic Studies (IBCS) at Xavier University of Louisiana, the only historically black and Catholic university in the nation, was a second home for Thea. It was while teaching there that she continued to gain notoriety for her popular and engaging classes. "The Institute," as it remains commonly known, was founded in 1980 and still offers programs in pastoral theology, religious education, and pastoral leadership and ministry. It provides an intellectual, spiritual, and cultural immersion in the black Catholic experience for all those interested in or committed to ministry in the black Catholic community.

Thea taught at the IBCS from 1982 until 1988. Her presence, charismatic personality, scholarship, and spirituality, along with the stellar skills, knowledge, and talents of her fellow faculty members, beckoned students from across the country to attend the intensive and academically rigorous three-week summer sessions. Word of what was happening during the summers on the campus of Xavier University in New Orleans spread fast, and people flocked to enter the program. At times, there was even a waiting list to enroll. The professors were demanding because it was important that the students learned accurately the history, theology, spirituality, psychology, culture, and aesthetics of black people.

Thea taught her first summer course at the IBCS in 1982, then hurried back to her parents and her work for the Diocese of Jackson. Her mother's health continued to deteriorate. Thea's schedule consisted of speaking engagements literally almost every week of the year, some in non-Catholic settings. For example, she was invited to give the keynote address at the annual Social Justice Day at Mount Canaan Baptist Church in Shreveport, Louisiana, on April 3, 1982. The theme of the day was "Let's Go Forward." Thea used stories from the Shreveport newspaper to cite some of the Reagan Administration's budget cuts and related them to how they would affect the poor. She said that funds to help children of low-income families and those living in substandard housing programs would be reduced. "The government is contemplating getting out of the substandard housing business altogether," she said. She also blamed society for being too judgmental on prisoners in penal institutions. "People say, 'If you do the crime, you have to do the time.' That's simplistic. Those people still have families."[16]

A common thread throughout many of Thea's speeches was to encourage people to use their God-given gifts and talents for the betterment of their churches and community and to build the kingdom of God wherever they find themselves. For several consecutive years she taught a liturgy and culture workshop in Washington, DC. During the 1982 workshop, she said, "Black people have developed their own way of worship, of seeing God. They read Scriptures and relate it to their own experience in this country. They are looking for the promise of a Messiah, they associate with the chosen people. The Church has called us to be ourselves. Part of our work is to challenge the Church universal to the diversity that is within theology."[17]

At the 1984 Louisville Archdiocesan Liturgical Conference, she admonished her listeners, "Make the liturgy come alive. Be colorful. Be bright. What we're talking about is freeing the spirit. We have to make the kind of joyful noises your children like to hear. That's how to free the spirit." She added, "One of the things black folk give to the church is freedom. My people have this thing—praise the Lord with your whole heart, mind and spirit. Freeing your mind and imagination is to see the good things the Lord has done for us."[18]

In New York City at the annual Catechetical Institute in 1982, she told the religious education teachers, "Faith is not taught, it's caught. We have to celebrate faith."[19] She let them know that she was initially drawn to the church as a teenager not by liturgy or theology but by the witness of a Christian community. "Little children don't understand all we say and do, but they will remember the witness of their parents and aunts and uncles. They will remember being part of a community of faith and love."[20] She told participants in a 1983 black spirituality workshop in Long Island, New York, "Black spirituality in America has always developed and been nurtured and shared. We've come this far by faith to recall together and share the spirituality that we are. That spiritually is the core of the Christian experience. Spirituality imparts a new dimension to the believer's life, affecting his or her relationship, morality, worship and most of all, daily living."[21]

In Beaumont, Texas, at the 1980 Southwest Liturgical Conference, Thea expounded on "Sacramental Celebration in the Black Community":

> The church was the newspaper where you collected the news about your neighbors every Sunday after services. The church was also the fashion show where you came to show off your new dress or suit—and you always came in late to be seen. The church was the economy institution. When a member's home was burned, the pastor would pass the plate for a collection to help the member to find a new place to live. The doors were locked and the plate was passed continuously until the amount of money the pastor had requested was raised. The church was the educational institution. The church was the political institution and this is where the civil rights movement began. As black Catholics, we need to see our own in a spirit of unity. We need to pray that God will send us our own priests, Sisters, bishops, directors of music to administer to our people and the Church. Until this comes to pass we are second-class Catholics.[22]

Thea accepted an invitation to present a paper on black spirituality at a Black Catholic Catechetical Symposium, sponsored by the National Black Sisters' Conference and held November 1–4, 1982, in Santa Cruz, California. Thea's presentation was titled "Spirituality: The Sign of Soul." Black spirituality, she told symposium-goers, is the God-awareness, self-awareness of black people. She guided her listeners through a stirring reflection that enabled the audience to better understand and appreciate the lived faith of blacks that is their spirituality. Among the other symposium presenters were cherished friends and colleagues of Thea, including Father Cyprian Davis, OSB; Sister Addie Walker, SSND; Sister Eva Marie Lumas, SSS; Father Giles Conwill; Dr. Nathan Jones; Father Fernand Cheri; Sister Toinette Eugene, PBVM; Sister Jamie Phelps, OP; and Father John Ricard, SSJ. One result of the catechetical symposium was the publication of a resource book on Christian education, pastoral ministry, and faith development called *Tell It Like It Is: A Black Catholic Perspective on Christian Education.*[23]

Among the media coverage of Thea's activities, some amusing headlines certainly captured her spirit, joy, and directness, including these: "My First Catechist Was My Granddaddy," "Catechesis does not have to be dull," "Sister Thea Bowman tells it like it is," and "Sister Thea Bowman: She enjoys her blackness." One reporter, Frank Wessling from Davenport, Iowa, conveyed his captivating experience after hearing Sister Thea speak by writing, "If you ever have a chance, go to anything that Sr. Thea Bowman does and let yourself be taken over by her. She is an educator with a difference, especially for white folks who grew up believing that colonialism was good for other folks."[24]

On February 13, 1983, she returned to La Crosse to become the first recipient of the La Crosse Diocesan Justice and Peace Award. The ceremony was held in Stevens Point, Wisconsin. Undoubtedly, she thought about her time in that city as a teenager recovering from tuberculosis. La Crosse Bishop Frederick Freking presented her with a plaque and a $1,000 gift to be designated for a charity of her choice. Thea designated the gift to Villa Infantil, an orphanage in Zaragoza, El Salvador.[25]

With her busy schedule, Thea was barely able to make time to celebrate her twenty-fifth anniversary as a Franciscan Sister of Perpetual Adoration. In June 1983, she went back to the FSPA motherhouse in La Crosse to celebrate with her profession class and the community. Twenty-five years after her profession, she was still the only black woman who had joined the Franciscan Sisters of Perpetual Adoration. In reflecting with biographer Margaret Walker some years later, Thea named the grace of her perseverance as a FSPA:

> When I think FSPA, actually I think of people who have enabled me. I think of some of the early FSPAs who came to my hometown, Canton, Mississippi, as missionaries. . . . They came into my world and showed me the possibility for life and growth that I had not ever dreamed of. They showed me that people from different races and cultures could work together and could enjoy it. . . .
>
> I would like to say from my heart: thank you to all the people who have been so good to me. I'd like to say I'm sorry for the times when I haven't connected properly. I'd like to say that there is still hope that we still can have good news and that we can still be good news for one another and that I think it's worth the effort.[26]

The FSPA motherhouse's profession anniversary festivities were a full day of celebration, being reunited and rejoicing in the grace of perseverance in religious life. On August 7, she celebrated the anniversary at home in Canton with her mother and father who had followed her into the Catholic faith years earlier sitting fraily by her side at a Mass at Holy Child Jesus Church. A photo of a joyous Thea in her bright African robe sitting with her parents on the front pew of Holy Child Jesus Church appeared in the *Jackson Advocate* newspaper soon afterward.[27]

In August 1983, the Diocese of Jackson hosted the annual joint conference of the National Black Catholic Clergy Caucus, National Black Sisters' Conference, and the National Black Catholic Seminarians' Association. Naturally Thea was on the local planning committee. Writing in the diocesan newspaper, the *Mississippi Today*, Thea explained the significance of the diocese hosting the meeting: "One reason we are meeting in Jackson is because so many of us have roots in the South. We also want to examine the concerns and gifts of the area since so much of our history has developed here and so many of our people still live here. We expect 400 participants with a large number coming from Mississippi and several large black parishes in Louisiana. Some of the convention activities will be open to local people and this will present them an opportunity to get to know the black clergy, sisters and brothers better." Welcoming participants, Bishop Brunini noted that in attending a conference in the South, "many of you have come back to your roots. I know for some these have been bitter roots, but through travail and suffering and depravation, strong trees usually grow."[28]

Bishop Fernand J. Cheri, OFM, auxiliary bishop of the Archdiocese of New Orleans, and Thea's dear friend and student at the IBCS, recalled being a priest serving on the national planning committee of the joint conference in 1983:

[It] was one of the best ones we've had. I got to see a side of her [Sister Thea] as she spoke passionately about the problems of racism that she faced growing up in Canton, Mississippi, and working at Holy Child School as well as dealing with racist attitudes among some of her own community and among church people in the Canton area. We planned that conference with the sense that she was going to showcase black religious for Mississippi. She gave us a taste of the Diocese of Jackson with all its gifts.[29]

Also attending the 1983 joint conference was then-Resurrectionist seminarian Manuel B. Williams. He had first met Thea when she gave a workshop in his hometown of Montgomery, Alabama, in 1980. After her presentation, he told her that he was thinking of entering the seminary and Thea had enthusiastically responded, "Good! We need you and I will be praying for you!" In 1983 he had just completed his first year of study at the IBCS and viewed the opportunity to be among such stellar black Catholic religious men and women not only a privilege but also an essential part of his priestly formation. He later recalled, "I remember she arranged a reception for us at the Governor's mansion, home of Governor William Winter, a new Southern Democrat. I will never forget that Governor Winter, his wife, and Sister Thea stood at the door of the mansion and welcomed every single participant of the joint conference. I remember several people from across the country saying, 'Here we are, a bunch of black Catholics in the governor of Mississippi's residence, and he's greeting each of us personally. What kind of black nun is this? Only Sister Thea could arrange this!'"[30]

Thea compared the annual conference to "a family meeting where everyone is free to openly discuss issues and problems. . . . I always look forward to these conferences. They are renewing for me. It's like a family reunion."[31] She was pleased that she was able to host her "family" in what was deemed a most successful conference.

During the early 1980s, Thea gradually transitioned from wearing the skirts and blouses that many sisters wore who were not in traditional habits to wearing traditional African robes. Her childhood friend Flonzie Brown-Wright humorously recalled visiting her at the convent in Canton one day and when she opened the door, Flonzie was shocked to see her friend no longer dressed in "traditional sister clothes." She asked Thea, what happened? Thea responded, "Girl, them petticoats were too hot!"[32] In an interview with John Feister later, Thea gave the deeper significance of her wardrobe development: "I'm different! The clothes are an expression of my personality, an expression of my values, an expression of my history and culture, and my tradition. I'm a black, traditional person."[33]

In the spring of 1984, Thea noticed a lump in her breast and went to the doctor the next day. Thea wrote about her initial reactions and procedures with her friend Margaret Walker:

> I was diagnosed in 1984. When I had my first cancer surgery, my mother had been in the hospital for about six weeks. I was in the room next to her and I remember, by that time my mother was not speaking—so I went in to tell her that they had discovered a lump and I was going to have a biopsy and that if the biopsy showed malignancy, I was going to have surgery. I told her I was in the room next to her, and as soon as I got out of surgery, I would come and see her. Her blood pressure shot up. That told me she understood what I had said. I went to surgery and as soon as I got back, I wanted to see my mother. They would not let me go see her until my doctor said, "Let her go."[34]

Sister Dort was away from Mississippi when Thea received the disturbing news of her breast cancer, and when she returned, she visited Thea at the hospital. Dort recalled, "Mrs. Bowman was in one room and she was in the hospital room next to her. I asked Thea the question anyone would ask of someone in the hospital, 'Is there anything I can do for you?' Thea responded, 'Yes, move in with me and help me take care of my parents.' I said, 'Okay.'"[35]

CHAPTER SEVEN

Being Black and Catholic
(1984–1989)

What does it mean to be black and Catholic? It means that I come to my church fully functioning. That doesn't frighten you, does it? I come to my church fully functioning. I bring myself, my black self, all that I am, all that I have, all that I hope to become, I bring my whole history, my traditions, my experience, my culture, my African-American song and dance and gesture and movement and teaching and preaching and healing and responsibility as gift to the church.[1]

Sister Thea Bowman, FSPA

Sister Dort moved from the FSPA convent on Garrett Street to join the infirmed Bowman family at their home on Hill Street. She continued her teaching responsibilities at Holy Child Jesus School while caring for Dr. Bowman, Mrs. Bowman, and Thea. She drove each of them to their scheduled doctor appointments in Jackson. She considered it an honor to be trusted by Thea to move into her home and become part of the Bowman family. Sister Dort later re-called, "I was very comfortable and made to feel comfort-able in the Bowman home. Eventually it became tedious with my school responsibilities and caring for Dr. and Mrs. Bowman and Thea, so without question my [FSPA] leader-ship team gave me permission to care for them full time."[2] This became her new ministry.

As Thea continued her chemotherapy treatments, she also continued her speaking commitments throughout the na-tion. In June she returned to teaching at the Institute for Black Catholic Studies at Xavier University. Among her students was School Sister of Notre Dame, Addie Lorraine Walker. Addie and Thea had a close and immediate bond. Before the meeting, their mutual friend, Trinitarian Father John Ford, had told Sister Addie, "When you meet her, you'll know her from the inside out . . . when you meet her you are going to meet yourself."[3] Sister Addie met Thea at a National Black Sisters' Conference meeting in 1980. Addie recalled, "It was really kind of frightening . . . and I think it was kind of scary for her, too, initially."[4] It wasn't long before these two like-minded and spiritually attuned black sisters formed an unbreakable bond.

Thea would be instrumental in both Sister Addie Walker and Sister Eva Lumas attending the newly created Institute at Xavier. They were among the first students to attend. Sister Eva Lumas recalled a course on the spirituality of black literature that Sister Thea taught at the Institute, and which both she and Sister Addie attended. She said:

> The first day of class she rattled off the requirements of the class and what she expected of us and the methodology she was going to use to explore the spirituality of certain Afri-can American writers and the spiritual themes within their

writings. Addie and I looked at each other and thought, "Oh Lord, do we really want to do this?" She and I decided that we were going to go upstairs at the break to the registrar's office and withdraw from the class. So we get upstairs to the registrar's office and Thea is there! And she says in her own inimical way, "What ya'll doing?" We responded, "Withdrawing from your class." She asked, "Why ya'll want to do that?" We said, "Because we want to be sane by the time we leave here." And Thea said, "Well, why don't you teach me how to teach you?" And of course that was news for me and Addie. She also said, "One of the things you need to know at the Institute is that we will not leave you hanging." And we decided that we would hang right on in there. We knew that she cared for the students![5]

The summer of 1984 at the Institute was especially exciting. What was initially a pilot program was beginning to produce stellar results, and the first three students were about to graduate with their master of theology degrees. Sister Addie from Texas and Sister Eva from California were the first graduates along with Father James Voelker, a priest from the Diocese of Belleville. The Institute for Black Catholic Studies' commencement exercises was the culminating event for the 1984 joint conference of black Catholic organizations, held in New Orleans. Black Catholic clergy, sisters, brothers, permanent deacons and their wives, and seminarians from across the country celebrated the first graduating class of the only graduate program in Black Catholic Studies in the nation. Sister Thea was the commencement speaker and gave a stirring oration, combining intellectual lucidity and spiritual passion as she expounded on the rich heritage of being black and Catholic.

On September 9, 1984, the feast of St. Peter Claver, the then ten black Catholic bishops in the United States issued a pastoral letter titled, "What We Have Seen and Heard": A Pastoral Letter on Evangelization from the Black Bishops of the United States. The black bishops seized the momentum that was building among black Catholics across the country to encourage them to continue to share their cultural gifts, the prophetic witness of their faith and faithfulness, and their readiness to evangelize within the black community and beyond. This declaration must have overjoyed Sister Thea, and she was very proud that her black shepherds had spoken on behalf of their people to say that they are no longer a mission people or a mission church but they, too, had the richness of their culture and faith to give as gift to the greater church.

The founding of black Catholic clergy and religious women organizations, the theological and pastoral publications of the Black Catholic Theological Symposium, the establishment of the Institute for Black Catholic Studies, and the prophetic pastoral letter of the black Catholic bishops all invigorated and spurred both momentum and action among black Catholics in the United States. The 1980s witnessed the appearance of the Kujenga (a Swahili word meaning "to build together") retreats for black Catholic youth. The reemergence of the National Black Catholic Congress (NBCC) called black Catholics to assume leadership and to evangelize in their dioceses and parishes. The NBCC set forth a pastoral plan for black Catholics initially through decisive deliberations and resolutions. They also held annual "pastoring in the black Catholic community" workshops for clergy and religious ministering in black parishes. It was a time of spiritual revival for black Catholics both figuratively and literally. There were parish and diocesan revivals preached at packed churches throughout the country by dynamic black Catholic clergy and religious women and men. Black Catholic scholars and theologians were making their mark on the church and society in various academic disciplines. Thea Bowman singularly was involved in most if not all of these important developments during the last decade of her life.

And yet while in her public life, Sister Thea was energized by the life-giving activities and ministries that surrounded her, her personal reality was the impending deaths of her beloved parents. By the fall of 1984, her mother's health was rapidly declining. Thea curtailed her speaking engagements because she knew her death was imminent. She and Sister Dort and the visiting nurse simply tried to make Mrs. Bowman comfortable as she laid awaiting death in the hospital bed brought to their home.

Thea shared her concern for her father as he watched his wife dying with biographer Margaret Walker:

> In November 1984, when my mother was dying, my father's nurse, a white woman who was in home health care, did not believe that Daddy knew his wife was dying. My father was a doctor and had practiced medicine for fifty-four years. The nurse thought we should tell him, and I agreed. We sat in the living room and the nurse told him she thought my mother was dying. My father sat there, his face did not change, and he said, "Thank you." He said, "You have been very kind and I know that you have done everything you could do." That was all he said. Even then, the nurse did not think my father understood. I knew he did—that would be the way my father would respond. Wouldn't that be a typical way for a gentleman to respond?[6]

At the age of eighty-one, Mary Esther Coleman Bowman passed away on November 15, 1984. Dr. Bowman had suffered a stroke and was in the hospital when his beloved wife died. He did not attend his wife's funeral. Thea knew her father was grief-stricken about his wife's sickness and death. A month and a day after Mrs. Bowman's death, Dr. Theon Edward Bowman died, on December 16, 1984. When her father died at home, Sister Dort said, "Thea just held her father's hand and talked to him. She told him that she didn't expect him to leave her so soon. She told him that she loved him and to go be at peace with Mama."[7]

Thea grieved deeply the passing of her mother and father. Sister Dort remembered, "She felt lonely and alone when her parents died. Thea had friends all over the country and that was a comfort to her, but she missed her parents—she missed having her family as she knew it. However, Thea began to view me more as her sister and she became very close to my family. She really appreciated all the letters and telephone calls she received from around the world. She also enjoyed keeping in touch with all of her friends, especially through her annual Christmas letter."[8]

In her "form" letter sent to friends, she conveyed her feelings about her parents' deaths: "I miss them, truly, but I trust, believe, know they are happy together with God and with so many loved ones who have gone before. Through it all, rightly, or wrongly, God knows, I've tried to walk and work on as if my world was steady."[9]

Incredibly, while caring for her parents, teaching, and traveling from coast to coast speaking, she was editing a book. She was concerned about sustaining and advancing the black family in America. She addressed this concern in many of her speeches. The US Catholic Conference commissioned her to edit a book on the black Catholic family. Thea entitled the book, *Families: Black and Catholic, Catholic and Black*. The book, published in 1985, was creatively comprised of articles and essays, admonitions and aphorisms, prose and poetry, litanies and para-liturgies, prayers and plans, songs, gestures, family activities and fun activities from black Catholic scholars, pastoral leaders, poets, and writers. A cursory review of the table of contents immediately shows that Thea mostly called on her friends to share their unique abilities, insights, and expertise. She had the uncanny facility to ask in such a way that her friends knew that her request wasn't a polite invitation but a tacit expectation.

Being an only child, close friends were her family without distinction. Thea dedicated her book to her parents, other family members, and Father Joseph Roy Nearon, SSS, founding director of the IBCS who had recently died. Thea was honored that her dear friend, Bishop James P. Lyke, OFM, PhD, then auxiliary bishop of Cleveland, wrote the foreword. Lyke noted that the book "is a welcome and significant contribution to the life of the Church in the Black community precisely because it is an affirmation of a family life, as well as an instrument to develop and sustain this life. The support is particularly needed at this time because the state of family life within our nation and within the Black community is experiencing serious difficulties."[10]

In her introduction of the book, Thea sought to be inherently clear regarding the book's purpose and import. She wrote, "It encourages Black families to think and talk about ourselves: our faith; our lived experience of family, Blackness, and Catholicism. It encourages us to think and talk about our dreams, goals, and aspirations; our concrete plans for being family and community, and for sharing our gift of Blackness with the Church."[11]

Among her myriad of commitments, Thea enjoyed teaching at the Institute. She taught the Spirituality of Black Literature, Black Religion and the Arts, and Preaching I and II on a rotating basis. As an educator, Thea's pedagogy was to motivate her students to be self-determined and inquisitive learners. On more than one occasion while teaching, she would abruptly stop the lecture to make sure that her students were not merely memorizing material, but fully comprehending and internalizing the lesson. She would quip, "So what does preaching have to do with your life, your family, your community, your ministry, or your lived experience?" She would stare at the class waiting for a response; her questions were almost never rhetorical. She demanded that her class of adult learners fully participate. There were no spectators in her classes.

Her educational stratagems humorously included trying to get her students to realize that they were both learners and teachers in her class. She would ask the ambiguous, yet loaded question, "Who's teaching this class?" If her students responded, "You're teaching this class," she would then ask, "Are you sure? Am I teaching this class or are you teachers as well?" The point she was impressing upon her students was that in the educational process—through dialogue, examination, and exploration—we learn from one another. She wanted her students to be confident that in the learning environment they were both learners and teachers. "Each one, teach one" was her constant mantra.

Father Manuel Williams, CR, recalled two courses she taught. The first was the Spirituality of Black Literature:

> She was a superb scholar, but she always managed to illustrate her points with vignettes, anecdotes, and stories that came straight out of the heart of Mississippi and Alabama and Georgia, that new Congo, that swath that came out of the black-belt in the deep South. The way she managed to teach her students was that she could rebuke you and point out the fallacy of some position you held, but she didn't make you feel badly. She would pull you along

until you found your way to an accurate answer. Her Spirituality of Black Literature course was incredible. The book we started with was the *Color Purple*, and I had read the book before, but under her direction and given insight I realized that I missed so much in the book. How did I read the *Color Purple* before and did not realize that this was a religious book? She made us see it.[12]

The second was Black Preaching:

I was delivering a sermon in a preaching class and my content was good, but my delivery was lackluster. And as she would typically do when something wasn't right say, "Stop! Manuel, stop." Then she asked, "What are you doing?" I responded, "Trying to preach this sermon." She said, "Something's not right with it." I stood there thinking, "What do I tell her?" Then she said, "You know what? You have beautiful eyes." First, I was shocked that she said it, and then I burst into this big smile. Then she said again, "Beautiful eyes. Now use those eyes as you're preaching this text to us. Use them to bring us in with it." And what it did was it made me relax. She could have went into a lengthy theoretical explanation, but all she said was that I had beautiful eyes, and I knew I had to make more eye contact when preaching.[13]

She often said to the students in her preaching courses, "How am I supposed to believe what you are saying if you don't believe it yourself? Preach with confidence and conviction, or sit down!"

In Thea's classroom, there was a long conference table; her students sat around the table, and she sat or stood at the head of the table. Once when she was teaching, a student whose mother had recently died was moved by something that Thea said in her lecture and began to cry softly. Being ever observant, she knew that the student's mother had died and continued to teach by walking around the table and in the midst of teaching broke out into song, singing the traditional Negro spiritual, "Sometimes I Feel Like a Motherless Child." By the time she was finished with the song, the entire class was crying, thinking of loved ones who had died.[14] Thea immediately began to process with the class what they were feeling and why, and the meaning of death, loss, and grieving. She was able to take exactly what was happening in the moment and make it a teachable moment.

Thea would often ask her students to self-evaluate, to give themselves a grade. Then she would look intently at the grades the students had given themselves and ask the students why they had given themselves that particular grade. If the students either overrated or underrated themselves, Thea would gently tell the students to "think long and hard" and reevaluate themselves. There were times when students would continue to underrate themselves and she would let the grade stand. This experimentation was a lesson in itself for her students, teaching them to be both truthful and confident in their abilities.

Per Thea's persuasive prompting, all black students at the Institute were discouraged from self-segregating in the cafeteria, chapel, classroom, and even after classes in the dormitory. She insisted that they share their culture and their stories with the white students attending the Institute. She admonished them to teach the white students so that they would learn and better serve in the black communities. If black students were congregating with their black friends, they would hide so as not to be reprimanded by Thea for breaking her rule. She constantly stressed the importance of helping others understand and appreciate the black cultural experience.

Thea had strong bonds of respect, admiration, and collegiality with her colleagues at the Institute. She was very close to Sister Pat Haley, SCN, who guided the seminarians and religious women formation program as well as the spiritual formation program at the Institute. Thea and Sister Pat were close and enjoyed one another's great sense of humor. They were both talented singers and would often lead the Institute community in song.

She also shared a sacred bond with Father Bede Abram, Franciscan Conventual from the St. Anthony of Padua Province. He was a native of Buffalo, New York. The bond between Thea and Bede transcended their shared blackness, Franciscan charism, intellectual prowess, depth of spirituality, and predilection for the dramatic. These two Franciscans were Francis and Clare anew. Their bond was the fact that they knew and understood each other in all of humanity's intricacies and complexities. Their shared experiences and capabilities to remain whole and holy was a gift of grace. While not much older, Father Bede respected Thea as a big sister, even when big sister had to challenge, chastise, and correct. Those corrective moments were ephemeral, and the bond remained intact.

Jesuit Father Joseph A. Brown, who would become a dear friend, teaching colleague, and IBCS director, met Thea in the final years of her life. They met in 1985 at the National Association of Black Catholic Administrators' annual meeting in Techny, Illinois. Father Brown had been invited to address the delegation. The priest-poet vividly recounted his first encounter with Thea:

> Just as the crowd fell into that universal quieting down that occurs at the beginning of every church service I have ever attended, a loud and raw moaning began in the back

of chapel. I could not help but turn to see what was erupting at that solemn moment. The same tall, dark-skinned woman who had disconcerted me at the reception was sitting in the last row of the congregants, rocking from side to side and uttering a truly unsettling vocalise. I asked one of my friends, "Who is that woman? She's dressed like a bag lady off the streets, and looks half crazy to me."

The response given me by Father J-Glenn Murray was a look of disbelief and shock.

"Do you mean you don't know who that is?"

"No. I've never seen her before in my life."

"That's Sister Thea Bowman," J-Glenn told me. He went on, whispering, "I thought everybody in the world knew Thea by now. People either love her or loathe her," he said. "I decided it was altogether easier to love her. So I do."[15]

Thea invited her new friend Father Brown to team teach the Spirituality of Black Literature course with her during the 1986 IBCS summer session. Students in the class reported that they thought that they had known each other for years and had done extensive preparation for the course, because they were spiritually, intellectually, and comically in sync. Their collective knowledge and love of African American literature combined with their staunch wit kept their students engaged.

Learning at the IBCS went beyond the classroom. During Thea's tenure at the IBCS, she always enjoyed a "field trip" to Dooky Chase's Restaurant in New Orleans. One former student recalled one of those experiences:

Thea's favorite place to eat in New Orleans was Dooky Chase's Restaurant. She would preface the trip with, "What you're going to see here is the finest in African American art. Leah Chase has a collection of art that make this not just a restaurant, but also a museum. It's a museum where we eat, tell our stories, so please notice what's around you. What you're going to experience here is art in our food. How it's prepared. The seasonings from Africa and the French influence and the Native American influence and the Spanish influence—it's going to be a veritable feast for your eyes, for your tongue and your ears. Don't miss it." And if that wasn't enough, in the middle of the meal, in this public restaurant with other patrons beside us, Thea would stand up and strike her operatic pose and burst into song. I had grown accustomed to Thea being Thea. I knew that's who she was and that was her gift. She was not a one woman show in the restaurant, but she pulled the consumers into her performance.[16]

There were several seminarians, both black and white, who attended the IBCS and whom Thea formed for their future priestly ministry through her scholarship, mentoring, encouragement, "mother's wit," common sense, and prayers. She would often say of her seminarian "sons" that "these are the priests I formed."[17]

When many of Thea's dear friends heard the prognosis of her breast cancer and that the cancer had metastasized, they wanted to do something special for her, realizing that she did not have much longer to live. They also knew that Thea was distraught at losing both her mother and father within a month. Knowing that Thea wanted to attend the International Eucharistic Congress to be held in 1985 in Nairobi, Kenya, her friends developed a "Send Thea to Africa" fundraising campaign. In a letter sent to the "Friends of Thea," then-Brother Joseph Davis, SM (he was later ordained to the priesthood), and Father Charles Burns, SVD, presented the request: "Over the years many of us have shared the gifts of Sr. Thea Bowman through song, poetry, narrative, and dance. As recipient, we have heard her express only one heartfelt desire—to go to the mother[land]! 1984 has been a painful year for Thea. Mother Africa in the presence of friends will provide much healing."[18]

In February of 1985, Thea received the devastating news that her friend and mentor, the founding director of the IBCS, Blessed Sacrament Father Joseph R. Nearon had died suddenly.[19] She had had time to prepare spiritually and emotionally for her parents' deaths, but Father Joe's took her by surprise. Mother Africa was beckoning Thea "home" to be comforted and cradled, to be renewed and restored, to be healed in whatever way "the homeland" wanted to bring healing.

In June of 1985, both Dort and Thea moved from the Bowman home back to the FSPA convent to live once again with their community. She was prescribed a regimen of megavitamin therapy and a strict diet to help prevent potential cancer cells from spreading. She had barely settled back into the convent before she resumed her hectic speaking and traveling schedule, and she looked forward with great anticipation to the planned trip to Kenya for the International Eucharistic Congress in August.

Nearly two hundred friends, colleagues, students, bishops, and even her friend Cardinal Bernard Law from Boston generously donated funds in response to the "Friends of Thea" letter.[20] Thea's travel itinerary included visiting a sister from her community working in Zimbabwe. Then she would travel on to the forty-third International Eucharistic Congress in Kenya. Fifty thousand clergy, religious, and laity came from all over the world to the African nation of Kenya to reflect upon and to celebrate the precious gift of Jesus Christ present in the Eucharist. Pope John Paul II traveled from Rome to be present and to celebrate the Eucharist with the Body of Christ gathered from every nation in the world.

Held from August 8 to 11, 1985, the Congress's theme was "The Eucharist and the Christian Family." Being a Franciscan Sister of Perpetual Adoration, Thea personally had a deep devotion to the Eucharist. The discussions, workshops, and major addresses on the Eucharistic piqued her interest and nourished her spirituality, rooted in her FSPA charism.

Besides her devotion to the Eucharist, being in the Motherland sparked a connection with a nation, a people, a culture that was foreign and yet familiar. Being the quintessential student, she enjoyed engaging native Africans she met in conversations. She loved learning and made poignant connections with her African sisters and brothers. Thea made immediate parallels with the African way of thinking, being, feeling, perceiving, and encountering God with her own. The connections were experienced in the hospitality, the food, the music and song, the cadences of the spoken languages. Unequivocally, Thea was home.

After the Eucharistic Congress, she and her traveling companions spent a few days sight-seeing, and then they traveled to the most populous African nation, Nigeria. A Nigerian religious sister whom she had met in the States and had stayed with her family in their home graciously received Thea.[21] Some days later, it was time to depart from Africa and to return home.

In a 1986 letter to friends, Thea reported, "My health continues even better than expected. Dr. Sanders removed two suspicious tumors in September 1986, both benign. I feel fine. Somehow God is not through with me yet."[22] It was good that she was feeling better, because the approaching demands on her time and her physical and emotional strength would be arduous.

That same year, she received a telephone call from Paul and Holly Fine, a married couple and producers of CBS's *60 Minutes* news program.[23] They were interested in doing a featured story about Thea's life, ministry, message, and battle with cancer. She agreed. She was informed that veteran news commentator Mike Wallace would travel to Canton to conduct the interview with her. Sister Dort remembered, "Knowing that Mike Wallace was doing the interview made Thea feel honored because he was considered the best. When the interviews began, Thea determined the locations for the taping of the segment. The one-on-one interview was taped in my classroom at Holy Child Jesus School. Thea insisted that Mike Wallace visit segregated Canton, especially seeing the differences between the black cemetery and the white cemetery."[24] The taping took place essentially wherever Thea was, including her speaking or teaching engagements in Canton, Jackson, and Raymond, Mississippi; New Orleans and Washington, DC.[25] Word spread fast throughout the Canton community that "Thea was going to be on *60 Minutes!*"

The CBS producers had learned that Thea taught Catholic priests how to preach, and they wanted to film her doing so. Though there were actually only ten or twelve students in her IBCS preaching course that summer, she made an announcement to the community that she needed every student who was a priest or seminarian to excuse himself from whatever class he had that morning and to report to the chapel in clerical shirts. Before a full chapel, Thea showed *60 Minutes* how she taught priests to preach.

The *60 Minutes* segment featuring Thea (titled "Sr. Thea Bowman: A Black Evangelical Nun") aired on May 3, 1987, to great acclaim. Among the highlights of Thea's comments to Wallace that it included are these:

> I think the difference between me and some other people is that I am content to do my little bit. Sometimes people think they have to do big things in order to make change.

If each one of us would light the candle, we've got a tremendous light. . . .

Oh no, I don't preach! I witness. I testify. I share the
Good News of the Lord Jesus Christ. The priests can
preach. You know women don't preach in the Catholic
Church. . . .

Who you gonna listen to first, the official preacher or
your own mama? I think women have always had influence
within our own communities and always will. So if I can't
preach in the Church, that's all right with me. I can preach
in the school. I can preach in the home. I can preach on the
bus. I can preach on the train. I can preach on the street. . . .

Black is beautiful. You have to believe it. Should I try it
out on Mike Wallace? Black is beautiful, and then you take
your finger and point it at yourself and say, "I am beautiful." And some children have a hard time saying that. When
I say that I am beautiful, what does that mean? It means I
am caring. It means I respect myself. It means I am confident. When I work with children, I always say to the kids,
repeat after me: I am poised, and they go through that. . . .
I still didn't hear Mike Wallace say black is beautiful. [Mike
Wallace: "Black is beautiful!"] Amen![26]

Mike Wallace later reflected on his interview with Sister
Thea in the foreword he wrote to a book of her collected
writings, *Sister Thea Bowman: Shooting Star*:

I don't remember when I've been more moved, more en-
chanted by a person whom I've profiled, than by Sister
Thea Bowman. I confess I was a little skeptical when she
was first suggested to me by Paul and Holly Fine, the doc-
umentarians who introduced us, but just one session with
this remarkable individual convinced me; her openness,
her compassion, her intelligence, her optimism, her humor
captured me. You simply couldn't come away from a ses-

sion with Sister Thea without sharing the special sense of joy she seemed to bring to everything she turned her hand to. . . .

Halfway into our filming, I learned that Sister Thea was already fighting cancer, but I couldn't believe it, for she was so confident, so optimistic, so determined. . . .

"But there aren't enough Sister Theas around," I told her. "One's enough," she promptly answered, "you ask my friends. They'll tell you that's plenty." She was wrong. For I was one of her friends, and we need so many more like Sister Thea.[27]

Thea was now an international celebrity, although she would never consider herself as such. Sister Dort recalled when her own father passed, she was with Thea during her summer course at Xavier University in New Orleans. Dort said:

I was feeling very sad about my father's passing, and Thea asked me if there was anything that she could do. I asked her to drive to Wisconsin with me for my father's funeral, and she did. After the funeral, she had to get back to New Orleans to teach her class, so she decided to fly back from central Wisconsin. However, she forgot her driver's license and would not be able to board the plane. When she told the ticket agent at the airport that she didn't have her driver's license, he said, "That's okay, I know who you are. I saw you on *60 Minutes*."[28]

In a striking coincidence, just weeks after the *60 Minutes* interview aired, the National Black Catholic Congress, a movement and organization established in 1889 to improve and enrich the lives of African American Catholics, re-emerged after being dormant for ninety-three years. Congress V had been held in Baltimore in 1894. Congress VI was convened in Washington, DC, from May 21 to 24,

1987. Fifteen hundred black Catholic delegates from 110 dioceses gathered on the campus of the Catholic University of America. The historic summit, whose theme was "The Development of Our Pastoral Vision," examined the cultural identity of black Catholics and their priorities for developing effective ministries aimed at nourishing and increasing the church's black membership.

Thea was invited to give one of the major addresses at the Congress, titled, "History and Culture." Being back on the university campus where her black cultural consciousness evolved and flourished in the early seventies, Thea spoke with a sense of urgency to the delegates:

> When we know who we are and claim the history, we claim the struggle, the pain, the challenge, the purpose, the journey, and the dream. We are who we are and whose we are because of all our journeys, and the children that belong to our communities are enriched because of a pluralism that reflects life in a world that is pluralistic. Do we know all we can know, of ourselves, of our history, of our arts, and of our experience, of our goals and of our values, the full range of what has made us a people? When we know and understand, then we can do what we need to do to help ourselves.[29]

Tangible evidence that supported the black Catholic bishops' declaration that the black Catholic community had finally "come of age" was the 1987 publication of *Lead Me, Guide Me: The African American Catholic Hymnal*, a collection of three hundred traditional and contemporary hymns, forty-eight seasonal psalm refrains, and four complete liturgical Mass settings and several acclamations that were representative of the black Catholic worship experience. The project had been the desire of Bishop James P.

Lyke, OFM, and others concerned with liturgical music in black Catholic parishes across the country. Its publication was a pivotal point in the maturation and advancement of black Catholic leadership and determination.

Bishop Lyke fittingly asked his dear friend and fellow Franciscan, a troubadour in her own right, to bless the new hymnal with one of two introductions. Titled "The Gift of African American Sacred Song," Thea's contribution was both a scholarly, historical treatise on sacred music and a riveting commentary that celebrated the creative genius of black people. She wrote:

> From the African Mother Continent, African men and women, through the Middle Passage, throughout the Diaspora, to the Americas, carried the African gift and treasure of sacred song. To the Americas, African men and women brought sacred songs and chants that reminded them of their homelands and that sustained them in separation and in captivity, songs to respond to all life situations, and the ability to create new songs to answer new needs. . . .
> Black sacred song has been at once a source and an expression of Black faith, spirituality and devotion. By song, our people have called the Spirit into our hearts, homes, churches, and communities.[30]

Not only was *Lead Me, Guide Me* a celebrated addition to black Catholic worship throughout the nation, it also inspired and encouraged black Episcopalians and black Lutherans to subsequently publish unique African American hymnals as well.

Yet another historic event occurred in 1987 for black Catholics. A historic pastoral visit of Pope John Paul II to the United States included a meeting with black Catholics from across the nation at the New Orleans Superdome on September 12. It was an especially significant moment for the black Catholic bishops, who had places of honor with the Holy Father on stage and were each personally greeted by him. Pope John Paul's message to black Catholics was succinct and hopeful. He concluded his remarks by encouraging his audience to share their cultural gifts with the universal church:

> Dear brothers and sisters: *your black cultural heritage enriches the Church* and makes her witness of universality more complete. In a real way *the Church needs you, just as you need the Church,* for you are part of the Church and the Church is part of you. As you continue to place this heritage at the service of the whole Church for the spread of the Gospel, the Holy Spirit himself will continue through you his work of evangelization. With a joyful and a hopeful heart, I entrust you and the whole black community to the loving care of Mary, Mother of our Savior. May she, who both listened to the word and believed in it, guide your lives and those future generations of black Catholics within the one People of God, the one Mystical Body of Christ. Through her intercession may grace be to all of you "who love our Lord Jesus Christ with unfailing love" (Eph 6:23).[31]

Before John Paul II departed the stage, Thea approached the microphone, to the applause, joy, and adulation of those gathered, to sing a stirring rendition of "Lord, I Want To Be A Christian."

Thea's appearance on *60 Minutes* caught the attention of singer and actor Harry Belafonte, who became determined to produce a feature film on Thea's life. Belafonte wanted Whoopi Goldberg to star in the role of Thea. Arrangements were made for Thea to travel to California to discuss the project. The world of Hollywood was new to Thea, but she was cautious and meticulous in considering all the details of the initial negotiations with Belafonte, including obtaining an agent and lawyer to represent her in the negotiations. Thea was aware of Belafonte's work on behalf of the poor, justice issues, and humanitarian causes, and she felt she could trust him to portray her in an appropriate and meaningful manner. He felt that Thea's life story needed to be shared with a wider audience because she embodied the hope and need for racial understanding and reconciliation so needed in the world.

Thea, by now often confined to a wheelchair, invited Belafonte to her home in Canton and then to the IBCS in New Orleans during the summer of 1988. He visited both places. In Canton, he met her friends, who shared stories of Thea growing up in Canton and the impact she and her parents had made on the community. The IBCS student body—which had grown to 160 students, thanks in part to the notoriety of the *60 Minutes* broadcast—was thrilled about Belafonte's visit. He felt very much at home on the campus of Xavier University, sharing time with the students and visiting classrooms. Thea wanted Belafonte to experience the uniqueness of the Institute and hosted a party in his honor in the lobby of St. Joseph's Dormitory. The students sang songs, recited poetry, and performed dramatic skits for the guest of honor.

On hand for the occasion was a newspaper reporter from the New Orleans *Midtown Picayune*, Mary Queen Donnelly, on assignment writing about Thea's life. The article she wrote recounted the excitement of Belafonte's IBCS visit and noted that he had helped Thea by pushing her along in her wheelchair. Donnelly quoted Thea as saying, "You see, we don't want to change the theology of the Church. We just want to express that theology within the roots of our black spiritual culture."[32] Donnelly later recalled her interview with Thea, saying, "Well, you don't have a sit-down interview with Thea. She wanted me to literally attend the Institute so she had me follow her around campus and interact with the students in classes and in between she would let me actually interview her. During that time, the Jesuits at Loyola University had invited her to come for a special Mass on their campus but Thea told them, no come to my house [at Xavier] and worship with me. She wanted others to come and have an authentic experience with black people. Thea didn't believe in the theory of the 'melting pot.' She believed that every ethnic group should be themselves."[33]

Belafonte's proposed movie on Thea's life never materialized; a screenplay was drafted but movie production never began. Belafonte's contractual right to produce Thea's story eventually expired.

Thea's dear friend Sister Norma Angel and Maryknoll sisters in Kenya invited Thea to lead a workshop in Tanzania in September 1988 for the sisters on racism. They encouraged her to bring a teaching partner to join herself and Sister Dort. Thea invited her former student and good friend Sister Eva Marie Lumas, SSS, to travel with her to Kenya. In turn Sister Eva Marie found funding to include Sister Marie De Porres Taylor, SNJM, to assist with teaching the workshops, especially if Thea became too weak to be present. Thea was overjoyed to return once again to the Motherland. The workshop was held at the Danish Volunteer Center in Arusha, Tanzania. Thea advised the Maryknoll sisters, who worked as missionaries, to stop speaking for the people and to encourage the people to speak for themselves.[34] Even before arriving, Thea had asked that every Maryknoll Sister bring at least one indigenous person to whom they were account-able. Only two sisters brought a companion, and Thea ad-monished the group not to minister as missionaries in an African country without having at least one African person to whom they would be accountable for the quality of their service and ministry.[35] Among the many people, places, and experiences of that African sojourn, Lumas remembered one experience in particular. She said, "Thea had us bring home a Baggie filled with African soil. And she asked us to please pour the African soil in her grave."[36]

The Daughters of St. Paul, who ran a Catholic publishing house in Boston, approached Thea about a recording proj-ect. She gathered her "singing friends," Leon Roberts, Ve-ronica Downs, Jerome Alexander, Ruby Ellis, and Melvin Gipson, to join her in Boston as her choir for the recording. Leon Roberts did the piano arrangements and assisted Thea with the vocal arrangements. Although sick and wheelchair bound, she was diligent in directing and perfecting every aspect of the recording. Veronica Downs recalled that it seemed as if singing brought life back into Thea's weak body. "She only took a lunch break and time to take an afternoon nap, after watching her favorite soap opera, *All My Chil-dren*."[37] The result was two cassettes. One was a collection of Thea's beloved spirituals entitled *Sister Thea: Songs of My People*. The other was a collection of Christmas spiritu-als entitled *Sister Thea: 'Round the Glory Manger*. Both products included a music accompaniment book. The re-cordings were a great success and she was pleased to share cherished songs of her faith and heritage.

In May 1989, *U.S. Catholic* magazine awarded Thea their prestigious U.S. Catholic Award for furthering the cause of women in the church. In presenting the award, the maga-zine's editor, Father Mark J. Brummel, said to Thea, "You know what a gift it is to be black. You know what a gift it is to be a woman. You know what a gift it is to be holy in God's sight. Thank you for teaching the church about the wondrous ways women have handed down a living faith from generation to generation. You teach how women have nurtured the faith, witnessed to that faith, lived it and died for it. You call on the faithful to honor that tradition, treasure it, and strengthen it."[38]

Thea was invited to give the commencement address and receive an honorary doctoral degree from Xavier University of Louisiana on May 14, 1989. Although increasingly weak, she gave a typically rousing speech to the class of 1989, to the delight of the audience. She told the graduates, "Be upwardly mobile, but make sure that what you're climbing for is worth having. What are you going to do to alleviate poverty? What are you going to do to teach the children, to comfort the elderly, to mold public policy for the betterment of the world? How will you serve humanity?"[39]

Less than a month later, she would give one of the most important and memorable speeches of her life. The cancer continued to ravage her body and now the cancer in her bones made it painful to move even in her wheelchair. People wanted to show their love and appreciation for the songs she sang or the sermons she preached by giving her hugs, but the pain was too excruciating and people had to be restricted from hugging her. Thea did not let her wheelchair or the deterioration of her body keep her from an unprecedented opportunity—that of addressing the US Catholic bishops. She was invited by the black Catholic bishops to speak to their brother bishops about the concerns and needs of black Catholics.

At their annual meeting held on June 17, 1989, at Seton Hall University, Thea spoke to the bishops as a sister having a heart-to-heart conversation with her brothers. In this well-crafted, yet at times quite spontaneous, message, Thea spoke of the church as her "home," as her "family of families," and about trying to find her way "home." She told them the "true truth" about what it means to be black and Catholic. She instructed and enlightened the bishops on African American history and spirituality. She challenged the bishops to continue to evangelize the African American community, to promote inclusivity and full participation of blacks within church leadership, and to understand the necessity and value of Catholic schools in the African American community.

In part, Thea also offered an explanation of a "mission mentality":

> Black people who are still victims within the church of paternalism, of a patronizing attitude, black people who within the church have developed a mission mentality— they don't feel called, they don't feel responsible, they don't do anything. Let Father do it, let the sisters do it, let the friends and benefactors from outside do it. That's the mission mentality. And it kills us, and it kills our churches. And so, within the Church, how can we work together so that all of us have equal access to input, equal access to opportunity, equal access to participation?
>
> Go into a room and look around and see who's missing, and send some of your folks out to call them in so the Church can be what she claims to be, truly Catholic.

And then she concluded,

> Now bishops, I'm going to ask you-all to do something. Cross your right hand over your left hand. You've got to move together to do that. All right now, walk with me. See, in the old days, you had to tighten up so that when the bullets would come, so that when the tear gas would come, so that when the dogs would come, so that when the horses

would come, so that when the tanks would come brothers and sisters would not be separated from one another.

And you remember what they did with the clergy and the bishops in those old days, where they'd put them? Right up front, to lead the people in solidarity with our brothers and sisters in the church who suffer in South Africa, who suffer in Poland, who suffer in Ireland, who suffer in Nicaragua, in Guatemala, in Northern Ireland, all over the world.[40]

And as the assembled American bishops stood with their arms locked at the elbows with one another, Thea led them in singing together "We Shall Overcome." When they finished, she received from them a thunderous applause and more than a few flowing tears.

At the end of her presentation she was presented with a beautiful bouquet of red roses. Her words of acceptance of the gift were just as profound as the stirring speech she had just delivered: "In the name of all the mothers and grandmothers, and aunts and friends, all the women who have brought you to priesthood, who have nurtured you toward episcopacy, who strengthened you in faith and hope and love so that you can be the Church of Jesus Christ, I accept these beautiful roses."[41]

The summer of 1989 was the first time that Thea was no longer able to travel to New Orleans to teach at the IBCS. Instead, the faculty, students, and staff, led principally by Sister Pat Haley, SCN, organized two busloads to go to Thea's home in Canton on July 4. Some students, keenly aware that going to Canton didn't absolve them of their homework assignments for the next day, reserved one of the buses for those needing to study. It had the moniker, "the study bus." It was decided that the students were going to share all that Thea had taught them. They gathered at Holy Child Jesus Church and paid tribute to Thea in song, dance, drama, and poetry.

Everyone present in the church that day knew that they were going to say good-bye to her, but no one said a word about her pending death. Children of the IBCS's participants presented Thea with roses. Thea made it somewhat comforting for everyone in her remarks at the end of the program, saying, "Thank you for giving me my roses while I'm still alive." Naturally, there were tears and sadness, but Thea smiled and thanked everyone as they came to her in her wheelchair to give her well wishes. Because no one could hug or touch her, they simply waved good-bye and blew her kisses.

Thea had begun discussions in 1984 with Dr. Leonard and Mary Lou Jennings, friends from Vermont, about establishing a college scholarship fund to assist disadvantaged African American youth in her honor. The mission of the foundation was to "establish the means by which to rekindle and enliven the hope and the opportunities which Catholic schools can offer black children."[42] While initially skeptical about establishing an educational foundation, the daunting vision became a reality as the Sister Thea Bowman Foundation was launched on October 19, 1989, at St. Michael's College in Colchester, Vermont. Thea, along with several university presidents and five bishops, was present to celebrate and encourage this newly formed educational endeavor. Besides the honor of the foundation being named for her, Thea received an honorary doctorate from St. Michael's College.

As the year 1989 drew to a close, the cancer dominated Thea's body completely and rendered her too physically weak for long-distance travel. She knew there was little hope of honoring the speaking engagements she had scheduled throughout 1990, often commenting that she would be there if her body let her. Thea knew that her time was drawing to an end.

CHAPTER EIGHT

She Tried (1990)

Life for a while and then death. It's as simple as that. When I first found out I had cancer, I didn't know what to pray for. I didn't know if I should pray for healing or life or death. Then, I found peace in praying for what my folks call "God's perfect will." As it evolved, my prayer has become, "Lord, let me live until I die." By that I mean I want to live, love and serve fully until death comes. If that prayer is answered, if I am able to live until I die, how long really doesn't matter. Whether it's just a few months or a few years is really immaterial.[1]

Sister Thea Bowman, FSPA

Thea's faithful friend and caregiver Dort knew that Thea was coming closer to the end of her life's journey on the evening of December 8, 1989. Dort later recalled, "It was one of the few times I saw Thea cry. The *Inside Edition* TV crew was taping a segment on Thea and Holy Child Jesus choir at church in Canton. Thea's voice cracked when she tried to reach the high notes she could always reach and

114

sustain to people's amazement. My heart sank; I can still see the look on Mr. Watson's face. Mr. Harry Watson was Thea's accompanist at Holy Child Jesus. That night, after our night prayers, she said, 'Dort, I couldn't reach the high notes today' and she sobbed. I just held her."[2]

When one comes to the end of her life, she often thinks back over her life. Thea thought back to her childhood. She had detested her birth name, "Bertha," and because of her size, other children often taunted and teased her. These unpleasant memories reminded Thea of the many lonely times during her childhood. While on a retreat in 1988, Thea had written a poem she called, "Only Child, Lonely Child":

> Only child, lonely child
> Daddy's kid, Grandpa's child
> Daddy's daughter, Mama's sweet little, poor little,
> black little lamb.
> Doris and Ada have 6 in the family.
> Ida has 11.
> May I go play over at Helen's house?
> Only child, lonely child
> Grandpa died Aunt Bertha died
> Charlotte died Joe died[3]
> Mama died Daddy died
> The Lord is my light and my salvation
> Thank God there's you[4]

Realizing that her health was steadily deteriorating, Thea said, "I believe that if He does not give me what I ask, He gives me something better."[5] On January 22, 1990, Thea wrote a "form letter" to her friends, updating them on her condition. While the news she conveyed wasn't good, she tried to remain hopeful. "My doctors are all conferring to decide if the best treatment will be radiation, chemotherapy, surgery or some combination. . . . I had to cancel all my January commitments, and what February will bring, God knows. I ask your prayers, I'm very weak, but my spirits are good and I'm trying to keep on keeping on. Again, I'm sorry for being so slow to respond to your generosity. Love, Thea."[6]

Friends from across the country called to check on Thea daily. Many times, she was resting and Dort would speak on her behalf. Close friends made visits to see her before she died. Those who could not come sent letters, greeting cards, flowers, and fruit baskets. This lover of the written language was no longer able to respond in writing to all the well wishes, so she solicited the help of Dort and other friends to write as she dictated her responses. Neighbors prepared meals encouraging her to try to eat to restore her strength.

In March, the Jackson diocesan newspaper requested that Thea offer a reflection to be printed in its upcoming Holy Week edition. In response, Thea dictated what would be her final meditation-reflection-sermon. She was on her deathbed, but Thea's words rang out with the fullness of life. She said:

> Let us resolve to make this week holy by sharing holy peace and joy with the needy, the alienated, the lonely, the sick and afflicted, the untouchable. Let us unite our sufferings, inconveniences and annoyances with the suffering of Jesus. Let us stretch ourselves, going beyond our comfort zones to unite ourselves with Christ's redemptive work. We unite ourselves with Christ's redemptive work when we reconcile, when we make peace, when we share the good news that God is in our lives, when we reflect to our brothers and sisters God's healing, God's forgiveness, God's unconditional love.
>
> Let us be practical, reaching out across the boundaries of race and class and status to help somebody, to encourage and affirm somebody, offering to the young an incentive to

learn and grow, offering to the downtrodden resources to help themselves. May our fasting be the kind that saves and shares with the poor, that actually contacts the needy, that gives heart to heart, that touches and nourishes and heals.

During this Holy Week when Jesus gave his life for love, let us truly love one another.[7]

Thea had died by the time Holy Week arrived, and the meditation was picked up by Catholic News Service and reprinted in Catholic newspapers throughout the country and Canada that week.[8]

Sister Celesta Day, FSPA, a registered nurse, came to visit Thea in her final days. On Tuesday, March 27, Thea made her final visit with her doctors in Jackson.[9] She went back home to Canton and prepared to die. She returned to her bed and the next day began to fall in and out of a coma.

Sister Dort recalled the day that Thea died:

It was five o'clock on Friday [March 30th]. I was wakened because Sister Celesta was moving around. I asked what she was doing. She said she was lighting a candle. I got up. Celesta said Thea's breathing pattern had changed. I sat on Thea's bed. She was almost sitting straight up to help with breathing. I put her right hand on my lap and held her. I asked Celesta if I could have a few minutes alone. Celesta left. I said, "Thea, it's Dort." She straightened her head and moved her shoulders and tried to open her eyes. I said, repeating like a litany, "Thea, I love you. It's ok to die. Your Mama and your Dad, Joe [Nearon] are waiting for you in heaven. Don't be afraid. It's ok. I'll miss you lots. I love you. Your friends John [Ford] and Jim [Lyke] say good-bye. We love you." I probably said that two or three times. I finally said, "I love you, Thea. Good-bye, Thea." Her head turned to the side; her shoulders dropped, her eyes didn't even try to open anymore. I asked Celesta,

Grace [Sister Grace McDonald, former FSPA president and archivist], Sister Addie Walker, SSND to come in.[10]

It was 5:20 a.m. when Thea entered eternal life.[11]

Thea had planned every detail of her wake and funeral. Her wake was held at Holy Child Jesus Church on Monday evening. She chose to be buried in her beautiful African-print garb with a single long-stemmed red rose placed by her head. Her frail body lay peacefully in a simple blue cloth-covered casket. An African corpse figure of Jesus with his hands outstretched was placed on the multicolored West-African kente cloth that draped across her casket. Thea wanted her funeral, her homegoing, to be truly a joyful celebration. The battle with cancer was now over, and she was at peace with the Lord.

Her funeral Mass at 11:00 the following morning was moved from Holy Child Jesus Church to St. Mary's Church in Jackson to accommodate the anticipated large crowd, which ended up numbering over a thousand people from every part of the country, crossing every economic and educational status, every ethnic group or religious denomination. Two of her closest friends officiated the funeral Mass. Father Bede Abram, OFM Conv, was the presider, and Father John Ford, ST, was the homilist. Also concelebrating in the sanctuary were Thea's friends, Cardinal Bernard Law, Archbishop Oscar Lipscomb, Bishop Houck, and many of the African American bishops of the United States.

Bede began the liturgy by exclaiming, "There's a woman I know, who challenged the people of her day. There's a woman I know, who allowed us to bear the name of black and Catholic."[12] The church reverberated with a joyful noise unto the Lord of gospel music and spirituals. Tears flowed down the faces of many who mourned Thea's passing and yet rejoiced that she was now with God.

Father Ford in his homily told the congregation:

> I asked Thea some years ago, "What do you want me to
> say, Thea, at your funeral? What can I say, in the midst of
> my tears, trying to understand who you were. What must
> I say, trying to understand the people who have owned
> you?"
> And Thea said, "Just say what Sojourner Truth said
> about her own eventual dying."
> "What was that, Thea?"
> And Thea said, "I'm not going to die, honey, I'm going
> home like a shooting star."
> Go home, Thea, go home.[13]

It was Thea's wish to be buried next to her parents at the
historic Elmwood Cemetery in Memphis, Tennessee. The
epitaph she requested was inscribed on her tombstone:
"SHE TRIED." After the funeral, Thea's dear friend Bishop
James P. Lyke, OFM, conducted the Rite of Committal at
the gravesite. Her friends Sister Eva Marie Lumas, SSS, Sister Marie De Porres Taylor, SNJM, Sister Addie Lorraine
Walker, SSND, Father Bede Abram, OFM Conv, Father John
Ford, ST, and Father Fernand Cheri all shoveled dirt onto
Thea's casket and poured the soil that had been carried back
from Africa less than two years earlier.

Father Fernand Cheri led the singing of "I'll Be Singing
Up There":

> If you don't see me singing down here,
> If you don't see me singing down here,
> Look on up to bright Glory,
> I'll be singing up there![14]

And one can easily imagine from her place with God,
Thea shouting, "Amen, Amen, Amen!"

Notes

Introduction—pages 1–8

1. The terms "black," "Negro," "colored," and "African American" will be used variously throughout this book to denote people of the African Diaspora, depending on the various time periods in question.
2. "Done Made My Vow to the Lord," African American Spiritual, public domain.
3. Interview with Joseph Smith, *Smith and Company*, WPTV Milwaukee Public Television, Milwaukee, WI, January 18, 1988.

Chapter One: Being Bertha Bowman (1937–1953)—pages 9–28

1. *Sister Thea: Telling Her Own Story* (Florissant, MO: Oblate Media and Communication, 1987), DVD.
2. Anthony B. Pinn, *Introducing African American Religion* (New York: Routledge, 2013), 37.
3. Ibid., 39.
4. Executive Order issued by President Abraham Lincoln on January 1, 1863, www.loc.gov/rr/program/bib/ourdocs/EmanProc.html.
5. Membership records of the national headquarters of Alpha Phi Alpha Fraternity, Inc., indicate that Theon E. Bowman was initiated in the Alpha Epsilon Lambda Chapter (alumni chapter) in Jackson, MS, April 1928.
6. Charlene Smith and John Feister, *Thea's Song: The Life of Thea Bowman* (Maryknoll, NY: Orbis Books, 2009), 12.

7. Ibid., 13.

8. Ibid., 14.

9. Ibid., 16.

10. Ibid., 18.

11. Ibid., 19.

12. The unopened 1928 bottle of Heidsieck Brut champagne is in the permanent Sister Thea Bowman, FSPA, exhibit in the Canton Multicultural Center and Museum in Canton, MS.

13. *The Bowman Family Baby Book*, Thea Bowman Collection, FSPA Archives (La Crosse, WI), cited in Smith and Feister, *Thea's Song*, 19.

14. Celestine Cepress, ed., *Sister Thea Bowman: Shooting Star* (Winona, MN: St. Mary's Press, 1993), 76.

15. Ibid.

16. *Sister Thea: Songs of My People* (Boston: St. Paul Books and Media, 1989), 7.

17. Smith and Feister, *Thea's Song*, 31.

18. Thea was baptized in the Episcopal Church as an infant. However, Father Furman, not having proof of her infant baptism, baptized her conditionally. Her baptism citation has been located in the baptismal records of St. Mark's Episcopal Church in Jackson, MS.

19. Smith and Feister, *Thea's Song*, 26.

20. Sister Mileta Ludwig, *A Chapter of Franciscan History: The Sisters of the Third Order of Saint Francis of Perpetual Adoration 1849–1949* (New York: Bookman Associates, 1950), 254, cited in Smith and Feister, *Thea's Song*, 31–32.

21. Ibid.

22. Pam Bauer, "Invitation to Sing," *Extension Magazine* 78, no. 7 (January 1984): 5.

23. Smith and Feister, *Thea's Song*, 33.

24. "She Inspires Thousands but Who Inspires Her?," *CUA Magazine* (Winter 1990): 7–8.

25. *The Non-Catholic in the Catholic School* (Washington, DC: NCEA, 1984), 20–25, quoted in Cepress, *Sister Thea Bowman: Shooting Star*, 92–93.

26. Thea Bowman Collection, FSPA Archives, cited in Smith and Feister, *Thea's Song*, 35.

27. Smith and Feister, *Thea's Song*, 36.

28. Author's telephone interview with Doris O'Leary, March 19, 2017.

29. Ibid.

30. Ibid.

31. Ibid.

32. Smith and Feister, *Thea's Song*, 37.

33. Author's interview with Flonzie Brown-Wright, Canton, MS, March 27, 2017.

34. Author's telephone interview with Doris O'Leary.

Chapter Two:
Becoming Sister Thea Bowman, FSPA (1953–1961)— pages 29–41

1. *Sister Thea: Telling Her Own Story*, DVD.

2. Judy Ball, "A Woman Wrapped in Courage," *Mustard Seed* (January 6, 1989): 1–2. As quoted in Smith and Feister, *Thea's Song*, 38.

3. Smith and Feister, *Thea's Song*, 42.

4. *La Crosse Catholic Register*, August 1953, cited in Smith and Feister, *Thea's Song*, 43.

5. Clarence Williams, CPPS, *Sr. Thea: Her Own Story: A Video Autobiography* (St. Louis: Oblate Media and Communication, 1991).

6. Smith and Feister, *Thea's Song*, 59.

7. Ibid.

8. Franciscan Sisters of Perpetual Adoration, "FSPA History," https://www.fspa.org/content/about/history.

9. Franciscan Sisters of Perpetual Adoration, "Mission and Vision," https://www.fspa.org/content/about/mission-modern-lives.

10. Smith and Feister, *Thea's Song*, 59.

11. Ibid., 62.

12. Bowman family scrapbook, Thea Bowman Collection, FSPA Archives, cited in Smith and Feister, *Thea's Song*, 62.

13. Smith and Feister, *Thea's Song*, 65.

14. Ibid., 70.

15. Ibid., 71.
16. Ibid.
17. Ibid., 74.
18. Ibid.
19. Ibid., 75.
20. Ibid., 76.
21. "Sister Thea Offers Black Experience," *Texas Catholic*, November 6, 1987.
22. Smith and Feister, *Thea's Song*, 79.

Chapter Three:
Returning to Canton (1961–1965)—pages 42–51

1. Interview with Joseph Smith, *Smith and Company*, WPTV Milwaukee Public Television.
2. Margaret Walker and Thea Bowman, *God Touched My Life: The Inspiring Autobiography of the Nun Who Brought Song, Celebration, and Soul to the World*, unpublished manuscript, Thea Bowman Collection, FSPA Archives, cited in Smith and Feister, *Thea's Song*, 90.
3. Jennifer E. Cheeks-Collins, *Black America Series: Madison County Mississippi* (Charleston, SC: Arcadia Publishing, 2002), 67.
4. "The Negro Needs Understanding," *La Crosse Tribune*, July 28, 1963, cited in Smith and Feister, *Thea's Song*, 91–92.
5. Ibid., 92.
6. Interview with Joseph Smith, *Smith and Company*, WPTV Milwaukee Public Television.
7. Author's interview with Cornelia Johnson, Canton, MS, March 27, 2017.
8. Ibid.
9. Williams, *Sr. Thea: Her Own Story*.
10. Interview with Joseph Smith, *Smith and Company*, WPTV Milwaukee Public Television.
11. Smith and Feister, *Thea's Song*, 93.
12. Ibid.
13. Ibid.

14. Interview with Joseph Smith, *Smith and Company*, WPTV Milwaukee Public Television.

15. Charles D. Burns, SVD, "Deep in Their Hearts, Lord, They Do Believe," *Divine Word Messenger* 42, no. 2 (March–April 1965).

16. Ibid.

17. Ibid.

18. Smith and Feister, *Thea's Song*, 96.

Chapter Four:
From Canton to the Nation's Capitol (1966–1972)—pages 52–60

1. Williams, Sr. *Thea: Her Own Story.*

2. Smith and Feister, *Thea's Song*, 100.

3. Ibid., 101.

4. "A Statement of the Black Catholic Clergy Caucus, April 18, 1968," in *Black Theology: A Documentary History, 1966–1979*, ed. Gayraud S. Wilmore and James H. Cone (Maryknoll, NY: Orbis Books, 1979), 322–24.

5. Lawrence Lucas, *Black Priest/White Church: Catholics and Racism* (New York: Random House, 1970).

6. National Black Catholic Clergy Caucus, "A Statement of the Black Catholic Clergy Caucus," 322.

7. See the history of the National Black Sisters' Conference at their website: https://www.nbsc68.com/.

8. Ibid.

9. Smith and Feister, *Thea's Song*, 104.

10. Ibid., 106.

11. Ibid., 108–9.

12. Ibid., 109.

13. Ibid., 110.

14. Ibid.

15. Ibid.

Chapter Five: Viterbo College: Professor Bowman (1972–1978)—pages 61–67

1. Williams, *Sr. Thea: Her Own Story*.

2. Smith and Feister, *Thea's Song*, 121.

3. Ibid., 123.

4. Ibid., 124.

5. Ibid., 125.

6. Ibid., 135.

7. Ibid., 113.

8. Grant Blum, "Soul Food, Dance Help Introduce Black Writing," *La Crosse Tribune* (La Crosse, WI), July 9, 1973.

9. "One Woman Show by Sister: Recital Sunday Night at Marian," *The Daily Sentinel* (Woodstock, IL), March 7, 1974.

10. "Singers to Raise Funds for School," *La Crosse Tribune* (La Cross, WI), July 19, 1974.

11. Susan T. Hessel, "Trip Is Experience in Hostility," *La Crosse Tribune* (La Crosse, WI), May 4, 1975.

12. The retreat reflection sheet that Sister Thea completed while living in the Murphy Center in La Crosse, WI, is in the possession of her dear friend and caregiver, Sister Dorothy Ann Kundinger, FSPA, who shared it with the author.

13. Smith and Feister, *Thea's Song*, 146.

14. Ibid., 146–47.

Chapter Six: Returning to Her Roots, Race, and Old Time Religion (1978–1984)—pages 68–85

1. Thea Bowman, FSPA, "Black History and Culture," *U.S. Catholic Historian* 7, nos. 2 and 3 (Spring–Summer 1988): 307–10.

2. Bill Minor, "Risk-Taking Bishop: Joseph Bernard Brunini," *New York Times*, December 25, 1969.

3. Catholic Diocese of Jackson, "Bishop Joseph Bernard Brunini," www.jacksondiocese.org/about/diocesan-history/growing-1853 -1977/1900s/bishop-joseph-bernard-brunini/.

4. John Feister, telephone interview with Bishop William Houck, November 19, 2007, cited in Smith and Feister, *Thea's Song*, 153.

5. Interview with Joseph Smith, *Smith and Company*, WPTV Milwaukee Public Television.

6. Ibid.

7. Smith and Feister, *Thea's Song*, 154.

8. Thea Bowman Collection, FSPA Archives, "Report on Progress on Inter-Racial and Inter-Cultural Awareness and Exchange" to Bishop Joseph B. Brunini, August 31, 1978, box 15, folder 10, cited in Smith and Feister, *Thea's Song*, 154.

9. "Fr. Clarence Rivers, Liturgy Pioneer, Dead at 73," *The Free Library*, *National Catholic Reporter* (2005), https://www.thefree library.com/Fr.+Clarence+Rivers%2c+liturgy+pioneer%2c+dead +at+73.-a0127432639.

10. *Theology: A Portrait in Black*, ed. Thaddeus J. Posey, OFM Cap (Pittsburgh: The Capuchin Press, 1978), cover page.

11. Ibid., 6.

12. Author's interview with Sister Dorothy Ann Kundinger, FSPA, Jackson, MS, March 26, 2017.

13. Author's telephone interview with Sister Eva Marie Lumas, SSS, May 3, 2017.

14. National Conference of Catholic Bishops, *Brothers and Sisters to Us: U.S. Bishops' Pastoral Letter on Racism in Our Day* (Washington, DC: United States Catholic Conference, November 14, 1979), 1.

15. "Sister Bowman Participates in Faulkner Workshop," *Mississippi Today* (Jackson, MS), August 21, 1981.

16. Victor Pizzolato Jr., "Sister Thea: Fight for Justice Has Been in the House of the Lord," *Church Today* (Alexandria, LA), April 14, 1982.

17. Mary Borrelli, "Afro-Americans Discuss Black Culture and Liturgy," *Washington Post*, September 1982.

18. Joseph Duerr, "Let's Have a Good Time in The Lord," *Mississippi Today* (Jackson, MS), October 19, 1984.

19. Claudia McDonnell, "Teaching the Faith," *Catholic News* (New York), October 31, 1982.

20. Ibid.

21. Maria Maloney, "Sr. Thea Renews Black Catholics with Song, Dance," *Long Island Catholic* (Rockville Center, NY), October 27, 1983.

22. Bob Giles, "Franciscan Nun Shows Liturgy Is Spontaneous," *Texas Catholic Herald* (Beaumont, TX), February 1, 1980.

23. National Black Catholic Sisters' Conference, *Tell It Like It Is: A Black Catholic Perspective on Christian Education* (Oakland, CA: NBSC, 1983).

24. Frank Wessling, "Not Your Average Learning Experience," *Catholic Messenger* (Davenport, IA), February 9, 1984.

25. *Stevens Point Journal* (Stevens Point, WI), February 14, 1983, 10.

26. Walker and Bowman, *God Touched My Life*, cited in Smith and Feister, *Thea's Song*, 176.

27. "25th Anniversary Celebration," *Jackson Advocate* (Jackson, MS), August 1983.

28. Thea Bowman, "Jackson Hosts National Black Catholic Convention," *Mississippi Today* (Jackson, MS), November 2, 1982.

29. John Feister, telephone interview with Fernand J. Cheri, OFM, St. Louis, June 25, 2008, cited in Smith and Feister, *Thea's Song*, 164–65.

30. Author's interview with Rev. Manuel B. Williams, CR, Montgomery, AL, April 15, 2017.

31. Cullen Clark, "Black Catholics Convene in First Southern Meet," *Clarion Ledger* (Jackson, MS), August 6, 1983.

32. Author's interview with Flonzie Brown-Wright.

33. John Feister interview with Thea Bowman, cited in Smith and Feister, *Thea's Song*, 178.

34. Walker and Bowman, *God Touched My Life*, cited in Smith and Feister, *Thea's Song*, 185.

35. Author's interview with Sister Dorothy Ann Kundinger.

Chapter Seven:
Being Black and Catholic (1984–1989)—
pages 86–113

1. Thea Bowman, FSPA, address to the United States Catholic bishops, "To Be Black and Catholic," *Origins* (July 6, 1989): 114–18.

2. Author's interview with Sister Dorothy Ann Kundinger.

3. Smith and Feister, *Thea's Song*, 170.

4. Ibid.

5. Author's telephone interview with Sister Eva Marie Lumas, May 3, 2017.

6. Walker and Bowman, *God Touched My Life*, cited in Smith and Feister, *Thea's Song*, 185–86.

7. Author's interview with Sister Dorothy Ann Kundinger.

8. Ibid.

9. Thea Bowman Collection, FSPA Archives, cited in *Thea's Song*, 185–87.

10. James P. Lyke, "Foreword," in Thea Bowman, *Families: Black and Catholic, Catholic and Black* (Washington, DC: United States Catholic Conference, 1985), 9.

11. Bowman, *Families: Black and Catholic, Catholic and Black*, 11.

12. Author's interview with Rev. Manuel B. Williams.

13. Ibid.

14. The author, Maurice J. Nutt, CSsR, was the student whose mother had recently died, and Sister Thea Bowman comforted him and knew of his pain having recently buried her parents.

15. Joseph A. Brown, *A Retreat with Thea Bowman and Bede Abrams: Leaning on the Lord* (Cincinnati: St. Anthony Messenger Press, 1997), 7–8.

16. Author's interview with Rev. Manuel B. Williams.

17. These seminarians included Glenn D. Parker, CSsR, Jesse Cox, OP, Manuel Williams, CR, Michael Kyte, OP, Maurice Nutt, CSsR, Brendan Cahill, Roy Lee, and Vernon Hugley.

18. Smith and Feister, *Thea's Song*, 194.

19. Ibid.

20. Ibid., 196.

21. Ibid., 197.

22. Thea Bowman Collection, FSPA Archives, cited in Smith and Feister, *Thea's Song*, 199.

23. Smith and Feister, *Thea's Song*, 199.

24. Author's interview with Sister Dorothy Ann Kundinger.

25. Smith and Feister, *Thea's Song*, 199.

26. Mike Wallace interview with Thea Bowman aired on *60 Minutes* (New York: CBS News), May 3, 1987. Reprinted with permission.

27. Cepress, ed., *Sister Thea Bowman: Shooting Star*, 9–10.

28. Author's interview with Sister Dorothy Ann Kundinger.

29. Bowman, "Black History and Culture," *U.S. Catholic Historian*, 309.

30. Thea Bowman, "Introduction: The Gift of the African American Sacred Song," in *Lead Me, Guide Me: The African American Catholic Hymnal* (Chicago: GIA Publications, 1987).

31. Pope John Paul II, "Meeting with the Black Catholic Community of New Orleans," September 12, 1987, http://w2.vatican.va /content/john-paul-ii/en/speeches/1987/september/documents/hf _jp-ii_spe_19870912_cattolici-new-orleans.html.

32. Mary Donnelly, "Nun Brings Black Roots into Church," *Midtown Picayune* (New Orleans), August 14, 1988.

33. Author's interview with Mary Queen Donnelly, Canton, MS, March 27, 2017.

34. Smith and Feister, *Thea's Song*, 234.

35. Author's telephone interview with Sister Eva Marie Lumas, April 17, 2017.

36. Ibid.

37. Author's interview with Veronica Downs Dorsey, New Orleans, April 3, 2017.

38. "U.S. Catholic Award to Sr. Thea Bowman," *The Catholic Advance* (Wichita, KS), May 18, 1989.

39. Thea Bowman, "Commencement Address," Xavier University of Louisiana, New Orleans, May 14, 1989, Xavier University of Louisiana Archives.

40. Bowman, "To Be Black and Catholic," 114–18.

41. Thea Bowman Collection, FSPA Archives, cited in Smith and Feister, *Thea's Song*, 262.

42. "Mission Statement," Sister Thea Bowman Foundation, 1989.

Chapter Eight: She Tried (1990)—pages 114–19

1. Fabvienen Taylor's interview with Sister Thea, "Lord, Let Me Live Till I Die," *Praying* (November–December 1989): 19–22.

2. Author's interview with Sister Dorothy Ann Kundinger.

3. "Charlotte" refers to Thea's friend and FSPA Sister Charlotte Bonneville. "Joe" refers to Father Joseph R. Nearon, SSS, Thea's friend and mentor.

4. Shared with the author by Sister Dorothy Ann Kundinger.

5. *Almost Home: Living With Suffering and Dying* (Liguori, MO: Liguori Publications, 2008), DVD.

6. Form letter mailed to friends dated January 22, 1990.

7. Thea Bowman, "How to Celebrate Holy Week," *Mississippi Today* (Jackson, MS), April 6, 1990, 7.

8. Smith and Feister, *Thea's Song*, 279.

9. Ibid., 280.

10. Author's interview with Sister Dorothy Ann Kundinger. Sister Dort gave the author her handwritten reflection on Thea Bowman's final days.

11. Smith and Feister, *Thea's Song*, 281.

12. Afi-Odelia E. Scruggs, "Music Fills Church as Nun's Life Celebrated," *Clarion-Ledger* (Jackson, MS), April 4, 1990.

13. John Ford, ST, "Funeral Homily for Thea Bowman," transcribed and edited by Christian Koontz, RSM, *Thea Bowman: Handing On Her Legacy* (Kansas City, MO: Sheed and Ward, 1991), 29.

14. Author's telephone interview with Sister Eva Marie Lumas, May 3, 2017.

Selected Bibliography

Bowman, Thea, FSPA. "Black History and Culture." *U.S. Catholic Historian* 7, nos. 2 and 3 (Spring–Summer, 1988).

————. "Cosmic Spirituality: No Neutral Ground." Address reprinted from *Formation in a New Age: Proceedings of the 1987 Religious Formation National Congress*. Washington, DC: Religious Formation Conference.

————, ed. *Families: Black and Catholic, Catholic and Black; Readings, Resources and Family Activities*. Washington, DC: United States Catholic Conference, 1985.

————. "Lord, Let Me Live Till I Die." (Fabvienen Taylor's interview with Thea Bowman.) *Praying* (November–December 1989).

————. "Let the Church Say, 'Amen!'" *Extension* (March–April 1987).

————. "Let Us Resolve to Make This Week a Holy One." *Mississippi Today* (Catholic Diocese of Jackson, April, 1990).

————. "Religious and Cultural Variety: Gift to Catholic Schools." In *The Non-Catholic in the Catholic School*. Washington, DC: National Catholic Educational Association, 1984.

————. *Sister Thea: Round the Glory Manger Christmas Spirituals* (compilation). Boston: Pauline Books & Media, 1989.

————. *Sister Thea: Songs of My People* (compilation). Boston: Pauline Books & Media, 1989.

————. "The Gift of African American Sacred Song." *Lead Me, Guide Me: The African American Catholic Hymnal*. Chicago: GIA Publications, 1987.

———. "To Be Black and Catholic: Address to the U.S. Catholic Bishops." *Origins* 19, no. 8 (July 6, 1989): 114–18.

———. "Trusting the Prophetic Call." (Catherine Browning's interview with Thea Bowman.) *Creation* (November–December 1989).

Brown-Wright, Flonzie. *Looking Back To Move Ahead: An Experience of History and Hope.* Canton, MS: FBW and Associates, 2000.

Brown, Joseph A., SJ. *Leaning on the Lord: A Retreat with Thea Bowman and Bede Abram.* Cincinnati: St. Anthony Messenger Press, 1997.

Cepress, Celestine, FSPA, ed. *Sister Thea Bowman: Shooting Star; Selected Writings and Speeches.* Winona, MN: St. Mary's Press, 1993.

Coffey, Kathy. *Women of Mercy.* Maryknoll, NY: Orbis Books, 2005.

Donnelly, Mary Queen. "Sister Thea Bowman (1937–1990)." *America* (April 28, 1990).

Ellsberg, Robert. "Thea Bowman." Chap. 30 in *All Saints: Daily Reflections on Saints, Prophets, and Witnesses for Our Time.* New York: Crossroad, 1999.

———. "Thea Bowman, African American Franciscan (1937–1990)." In *Blessed Among Women: Women Saints, Prophets, and Witnesses for Our Time.* New York: Crossroad, 2005.

———. "Thea Bowman—A Gift to the Church." Chap. 10 in *Modern Spiritual Masters: Writings on Contemplation and Compassion.* Maryknoll, NY: Orbis Books, 2008.

———. "Servant of God Thea Bowman." In *The Franciscan Saints.* Maryknoll, NY: Orbis Books, 2017.

Feister, John., ed. *Thank You, Sisters: Stories of Religious Women and How They Enrich Our Lives.* ("Those Preachin' Women" essay by Maurice J. Nutt, CSsR.) Cincinnati: Franciscan Media, 2013.

Harris, Kim R. "Sister Thea Bowman: Liturgical Justice Through Black Sacred Song." *U.S. Catholic Historian* 35, no. 1 (Winter 2017).

Hevesi, Dennis. "Sister Thea Bowman, 52, Worker for Catholic Sharing with Blacks" (obituary). *The New York Times* (April 1, 1990).

Hill, Brennan. "Thea Bowman." In *8 Freedom Heroes: Changing the World with Faith*. Cincinnati: St. Anthony Messenger Press, 2007.

Iozzio, M. J. "Liturgical Anthropology of a Soulful Sister: Thea Bowman, FSPA." Disability in the Christian Tradition. *Journal of Religion, Disability & Health* 17, no. 3 (2013).

Koontz, Christian, RSM, ed. *Thea Bowman: Handing on Her Legacy*. New York: Sheed and Ward, 1991.

Kosloski, Philip. "Thea Bowman's Cause for Canonization Endorsed by U.S. Bishops." *Aleteia* (November 15, 2018).

Leach, Michael. "She Who Overcame—Sister Thea Bowman." Chap. 28 in *Why Stay Catholic? Unexpected Answers to a Life-Changing Question*. Chicago: Loyola Press, 2011.

McBrien, Richard. "Saintly Figures: Bowman, Rahner and Climacus." *National Catholic Reporter* (March 23, 2009).

McCollum, Maureen. "The Legacy of Sister Thea Bowman." *Wisconsin Life* (July 13, 2015).

McGrane, Janice, SSJ. "Thea Bowman: Our Companion in Joy-filled Suffering." Chap. 10 in *Saints to Lean On: Spiritual Companions for Illness and Disability*. Cincinnati: St. Anthony Messenger Press, 2006.

McGrath, Michael O'Neill, OSFS. *This Little Light: Lessons in Living from Sister Thea Bowman*. Maryknoll, NY: Orbis Books, 2008.

Meehan, Bridget Mary. *Praying with Visionary Women*. New York: Sheed and Ward, 1999.

Nieli, Bruce, CSP. "Uniting America Spiritually." *America* (April 24, 2006).

Nutt, Maurice J., CSsR. *An Hour with Thea Bowman* (pamphlet). Liguori, MO: Liguori Publications, 2018.

———, editor and compiler. *Thea Bowman: In My Own Words*. Liguori, MO: Liguori Publications, 2009.

————. "Thea Bowman: Keep On Keeping On!" *The Journal of the Black Catholic Theological Symposium* IV (Astor, FL: Fortuity Press, 2010).

————. "Thea Bowman: The Courage To 'Live Until I Die.' " *Liguorian* (Liguori, MO: Liguori Publications, March 2010).

Parachin, Victor M. "Thea Bowman: Soulful Mystic." *The Priest* (June 20, 2011).

Pattison, Mark. "Bishops Give Go-Ahead to Diocese's Sister Thea Bowman Sainthood Effort." *Catholic News Service* (November 14, 2018).

Porter, Jeanne. "The Leader as Choreographer Highlights Thea Bowman's Life." Chap. 5 in *Leading Ladies: Transformative Biblical Images for Women's Leadership*. Philadelphia: Innisfree Press, 2000.

Pramuk, Christopher. "To Live Fully: The Witness of Sister Thea Bowman." *America* (June 24, 2014).

Roberts, Tom. "Good News for One Another: The Legacy of Sr. Thea Bowman." *National Catholic Reporter* (April 30, 2015).

————. Chaps. 1 and 11 in *The Emerging Catholic Church: A Community's Search for Itself*. Maryknoll, NY: Orbis Books, 2011.

————. "The Sister Who Preached 'True Truths.' " *National Catholic Reporter* (June 10, 2010).

Schaeffer, Pamela. "10 Years Later, Thea Bowman Still Inspires." *National Catholic Reporter* (March 24, 2000).

Smith, Charlene, FSPA. "Thea-logy: Memories of Thea Bowman." *U.S. Catholic* 75, no. 3 (March 2010).

Smith, Charlene, FSPA, and John Feister. *Thea's Song: The Life of Thea Bowman*. Maryknoll, NY: Orbis Books, 2009.

Tighe, Mike. "Playwright: 'We Need Thea Bowman' in a Troubled Time." *La Crosse Tribune* (September 2, 2018).

Williams, Shannen Dee. "Dear Hollywood, It's Time To Start Making Films about Real Black Catholic Nuns." *Religion Dispatches* (June 10, 2015).

Zagano, Phyllis. "Thea Bowman (1937–1990)." In *Twentieth-Century Apostles: Contemporary Spirituality in Action.* Collegeville, MN: Liturgical Press, 1999.

Index